Calling Clergy

OTHER BOOKS BY ELIZABETH RANKIN GEITZ

Fireweed Evangelism
Gender and the Nicene Creed
Soul Satisfaction
Entertaining Angels
Recovering Lost Tradition
Welcoming the Stranger
Women's Uncommon Prayers (co-editor)

Calling Clergy

A Spiritual & Practical Guide
Through the Search Process

Elizabeth Rankin Geitz

CHURCH PUBLISHING, INCORPORATED
NEW YORK

Library of Congress Cataloging-in-Publication Data
Geitz, Elizabeth Rankin.
  Calling clergy : a spiritual & practical guide through the search process /
Elizabeth Rankin Geitz.
    p. cm.
  Includes bibliographical references.
  ISBN 978-0-89869-543-4 (pbk.)
  1. Clergy—Appointment, call, and election. 2. Vocation, Ecclesiastical.
  3. Pastoral theology. 4. Pastoral search committees. I. Title.
  BV4011.4.G45 2007
254—dc22

                                                    2007003873

Printed in the United States of America

Church Publishing, Incorporated
445 Fifth Avenue
New York, New York 10016
www.churchpublishing.org

5 4 3 2 1

Dedicated to my colleagues in Transition Ministry
throughout the Episcopal Church,
with gratitude and thanksgiving

Table of Contents

*Note: Resources 1, 2, 3, 17, 18, and 19 are included in this volume.
All of the Resources may be downloaded from
www.churchpublishing.org/callingclergy.*

Acknowledgments

Many thanks to Mr. Frank Tedeschi, Executive Editor of Church Publishing, Inc., for urging me to turn my original diocesan search manual into a guide for parishes across the Episcopal Church. His insight and wisdom have been invaluable. My heartfelt appreciation goes also to my bishop, the Rt. Rev. George Councell, whose deep spirituality is instructive to me each and every day. His friendship, support, and guidance are a Godsend.

My thanks also to the Very Rev. Rebecca McClain, whose support for this project at the Episcopal Church Center gave me the courage to move forward, and to the Rev. Canon Matthew Stockard, who first saw the potential of a spiritual guide for discernment committees.

I also owe a debt of gratitude to the Rev. Paul Hunt, whose original Consultant Handbook served as the model for several of the sample meetings. Ideas for these meetings were also generated by the Rev. Alice Downs, the Rev. Richard Kirk, the Rev. John Powell, the Rev. Robert Ripson, the Rev. Dr. Molly Dale Smith, and the Rev. Craig Wylie, present and former Transition Consultants in the Diocese of New Jersey. Their collective experience aided greatly in the formation of these chapters.

My colleagues in the Ministry of Transition throughout the Episcopal Church have been an oasis for me in the midst of serving God in this ministry. I am deeply grateful to them. I would also like to thank Ms. Cecilia Alvarez, Mr. Michael Wilkes, and the Rev. Deacon Eric Elley, who as always were there to help with various issues as they inevitably arose.

Last, and never least, is my husband of thirty-three years, Michael, whose unfailing support of all my projects is a blessing to be treasured always—and our children, Charlotte and Mike, the sunshine in our lives.

O God, who has made us creatures of time, so that every tomorrow is unknown country, and every decision a venture in faith: Grant us, frail children of the day, who are yet blind to the future, to move toward it in the sure confidence of your love, from which neither life nor death can ever separate us. Amen.

— Reinhold Niebuhr

Introduction

When I share that I am writing a book to guide Search Committees through the process of calling a rector or vicar,[1] the responses I receive are as varied as the moods on a mood ring. In the midst of one such conversation at the 2006 General Convention of the Episcopal Church, a former Search Committee Chair emphatically interjected, "I'd rather have open-heart surgery without anesthesia than participate in that process again!" Another committee chair stated, "It was a rewarding, growing experience for me. I gained confidence through my personal and my congregation's spiritual growth."

What different ingredients contributed to these two contrasting experiences of the same process? While serving as Deployment Officer in the Diocese of New Jersey for the last seven years I have learned a great deal. I have seen some searches proceed smoothly while others have resulted in mayhem, both for the committee and the congregation as a whole. *Calling Clergy: A Spiritual and Practical Guide Through the Search Process* contains knowledge gleaned from my own experiences of the Discernment Process, along with the experience of some of my dear colleagues across the Episcopal Church who share this ministry with me.

Over the years I have observed one key ingredient that distinguishes searches which are life-giving and productive from those which are draining and nonproductive. The degree to which the committee focuses on the spiritual dynamics underlying the Discernment Process has an impact on every aspect of the search. Without a consistent focus on God and prayer, committees can easily become distracted by the many task-oriented challenges facing them. Without a consistent focus on discernment, members can allow other motivations to cloud their decision-making. For this reason, spiritual guidance is offered here each and every step of the way, through the sample meetings and individual spiritual reflections for committee members.

Another key ingredient to a positive outcome is focusing on the congregation's strengths throughout the process. This is not to say that serious issues in the parish should be ignored. They should not,

---

1. While this book is written specifically for Episcopal churches, it can be used successfully by any mainline denomination. For the terms "rector" or "vicar," substitute "pastor"; for "vestry," substitute "sessions," "board of trustees," or "governing board"; for "diocese," substitute "judicatory."

either in the Self-Study or in the Discernment Process. But it is to say that if the organizational development maxim is true that "what you focus on becomes your reality," then by all means let's focus on our strengths! You will find this belief highlighted in the sample meetings.

A third ingredient leading to a rewarding Discernment Process is following the diocesan guidelines set forth by the bishop. Churches that do so end up with the most appropriate candidates, experience less frustration, save time, and fare better in the long run. This has been true across the board. Diocesan guidelines are there to protect both congregations and clergy. Throughout this book, committees are consistently referred to their diocesan representatives for information unique to their particular diocese.

Intentionally, most diocesan processes uphold the principle of Affirmative Action. Yet the number of women serving as senior rectors is significantly and statistically lower than the number of men;[2] the number of clergy of color leading primarily white congregations appears to be less than one percent—a disturbing statistic given our baptismal covenant in which we strive to "seek and serve Christ in all persons" and to "respect the dignity of every human being."[3] Even though many congregations conduct an Affirmative Action search through the Episcopal Church Center's deployment office, it has not significantly altered the outcome of many parish searches due to the reality of systemic sexism and racism, which is alive and well in many institutions in the United States today, including the church. With prayers that this trend will be reversed sooner rather than later, there is a chapter addressing these and other "isms." In addition, an Anti-Racism Workshop is included and strongly suggested for all vestry and Discernment Committee members.

Language is likewise a significant ingredient in the Discernment Process in most mainline denominations, one that I believe is shaping that process in a manner inconsistent with who we say we are and who we strive to be. Language defines. Language shapes. Language teaches. During the writing of this book, I became painfully aware that the language we commonly use to describe the Discernment Process actually misrepresents and secularizes it.

I grew up in Clarksville, Tennessee, home of the 101st Airborne Division at Ft. Campbell. I regularly heard of troops being deployed to faraway countries to fight enemy soldiers. Little did I realize that over forty years later as an Episcopal priest I would have the title of Deployment Officer. Whom am I deploying, where am I sending them, and what am I sending them to do—fight? While church history

2. See Matthew J. Price, "The State of the Clergy 2006" (New York: Church Pension Group, 2006), 10 and 13, downloadable from www.cpg.org/productsservices/research/cfm.
3. I have written "appears to be" because there is not a comprehensive survey of this statistic available at this time. My own research involving questions of each Deployment Officer in the Episcopal Church produced this statistic.

throughout the ages may sometimes suggest otherwise, deployment of our clergy has nothing to do with this.[4]

Instead, it has to do with parish search processes in which clergy are interviewed by Search Committees for the position of rector or vicar of a congregation. Anyone who has worked in the business world is familiar with this terminology. In business, when a position becomes available a search process ensues in which candidates are interviewed. In this process, the candidate is being hired by a superior for whom they will work. There is a clear hierarchy involved, where one party holds all the cards. Why then do mainline churches of many different denominations regularly use this same language? Because at one point in history, the church adopted some of the language of institutional structures in America. Has this served us well?

From the very beginning of a Discernment Process, the language currently in use sets up unrealistic expectations in members of Search Committees, vestries, and congregations. The language of "search" and "interview" communicates to members that they alone are making a decision about whom to "hire." The language itself assumes an employer/employee relationship in which the decision-making is done by the committee or vestry, rather than by a process of mutual discernment between committee, vestry, and priest. The words convey a relationship and an attitude that is counter to mutual ministry. As a result, it can lead to future conflict between priest and parish, as well as confusion during the "search" itself. I have seen this happen time and time again regardless of how much my colleagues and I have talked about issues of mutuality in the process.

When a Search Committee decides on a final candidate for rector and that person accepts a call elsewhere, or simply declines the offer, the committee is often devastated. Why? Because there has not been enough focus on mutual discernment by both priest and committee throughout the process. This same mindset often flavors the priest/parish relationship going forward.

In recent years, attempts have been made to name this a "Calling Process" rather than a "Search Process," yet as long as the rest of the language used is either corporate or military in nature, confusion will continue. Therefore, after much thought and prayer, I have used different terminology in this book for each phase of the process. Instead of "Search Process" you will find the term "Discernment Process."[5] Instead of "Search Committees" you will read of "Discernment

---

4. As of the writing of this book, the Very Rev. Rebecca McClain, Executive Director of the Church Deployment Office, Episcopal Church Center, is in the process of changing the use of the word "deployment" to "transition" to describe the work of her office and diocesan offices throughout the Episcopal Church.

5. Why then is the term "Search Process" used in the subtitle of this book? Because its use is so widespread that not to use it would cause confusion as to what the book is actually about. My hope is that the change to the term "Discernment Process," or another phrase connoting the spirituality involved, will occur in part as a result of the process outlined here.

Committees," and instead of "Profile Committees," you will find "Self-Study Committees." A "Deployment Officer" is called a "Transition Ministries Officer," and a "Search Consultant" is a "Transition Consultant." An interview is referred to as a conversation, a meeting, or a time of mutual discernment. Since the language being replaced here has been used so consistently throughout the church, a chart has been provided on page 8 for easy reference as you read this book.

It is my prayer that as language shapes and defines, use of different language will give shape to a different process of seeking rectors and vicars in the Episcopal Church—one in which the primary task focuses on the Discernment Committee and the priest discerning God's will together as it is related to an individual parish. Each sample meeting and spiritual reflection is designed to support and encourage this process.

Yes, there are key ingredients in rewarding discernment processes that can be highlighted. Disturbing trends *can* be reversed through intentional education and prayer. And yes, language does define, shape, and teach. Let's begin shaping the process by which we call clergy to our congregations in a manner consistent with our Christian heritage. This is who we are. This is what we do best. Let's do it.

A Note for Vestry Members

You have been chosen to serve on your vestry during a time of significant transition in your congregation. You may have known that your rector or vicar would soon be leaving or you may have been taken completely by surprise. Whatever the case, you are now called to lead during this transformational time in the life of your church. And yes, it can be transformational.

You are about to begin or already are in the midst of an interim period.[1] One wise interim held a forum her first Sunday about the tasks of the interim time. On the wall behind her to the left a sign was posted that said: "Change is Inevitable." On the right was another sign that read: "Growth is Optional."

Whether or not your parish grows spiritually during this time of transition will depend in part on your willingness to lead through this period of change. Change is difficult for some people; they did not ask for it and do not like it. You will hear, "But the church is the one place that should not change. I need that constant in my life." Yes, but you are in the midst of a change in clergy leadership that will of necessity bring about change in the congregation. Once that process is set in motion, you cannot turn back the clock, regardless of how much that may be desired by some.

Working closely with your interim to discern the next best steps for your parish will be critical during this period. One of your first tasks will be to appoint a Self-Study Committee and a Discernment Committee. These individuals will shape much of what is to come in the life of your parish. For this reason, the one bedrock quality needed in every person who will serve in this capacity is that they are *spiritually committed persons of prayer.* And that is the bottom line. Whatever other skills or gifts they might possess, if this one key ingredient is missing, your Self-Study and Discernment Processes will be far less than they can be. I have seen gifted people serving on these committees who put their

---

1. For more information about the interim period, go to www.episcopalchurch.org/cdo and download *Interim Ministries: Book I* and *Interim Ministries: Book II.* To further prepare yourself for your role as a vestry member in the Discernment Process, the following booklets can also be ordered or downloaded: *Prayer in the Calling Process, Caring for Clergy through Housing,* and *Caring for Clergy through Compensation,* third edition. These booklets have been carefully prepared by the Episcopal Church Deployment Board and have been used successfully for many years.

own needs before the needs of the congregation, their own needs before the will of God. This is when a process can derail or ultimately not serve the congregation well; therefore, being a person of prayer is the first and most important qualification for people serving on either committee.

The Self-Study Committee will need people with specific gifts as well. Since they will be producing a profile, look at the overview on pages 25 and 26 and decide who in your congregation has the needed gifts to get the job done. If you decide to have a web-based profile (which I recommend due to cost and exposure), you will need someone who can design a webpage, for example. More and more churches are moving toward a computer-based process; people with these skills will be needed.

Your Discernment Committee will primarily and above all need people committed to prayer, willing to undergo the rigorous work of spiritual discernment. In addition, it is good to have different groups in the church represented on this committee. However, there is a caution here. The makeup of your committee will communicate a great deal to prospective candidates. One rector remarked that he had a skewed perspective of his current parish from the Discernment Process because each group in the church was equally represented on the committee, whereas they were not equally represented within the congregation itself. This is good to keep in mind. In addition, note that a Discernment Process is completely different from a corporate search, bearing little if any resemblance to it. Your local human resources person may not be a good choice for a Discernment Committee, as much of what she/he knows will need to be unlearned.

What about numbers? The recommendation in each diocese will be different. However, I suggest that in parishes with an Average Sunday Attendance of 150 or more, nine to twelve members serve on each committee, with three vestry members on each. In addition, three non-vestry members of the Self-Study Committee can also serve on the Discernment Committee to ensure continuity.[2] It is best for wardens not to serve on either committee, as they will have a distinct role later in the process. In parishes with an Average Sunday Attendance of below 125 people, seven members per committee can suffice, with the rest of the criteria the same. With attendance from 125 to 150, use whatever number works best for your congregation.

Another note of caution. It is best to be clear from the outset that each of these committees is a subcommittee of the vestry. They are not standing committees in their own right. Working cooperatively with the vestry is critical to a healthy, productive process. You are to produce a mandate for each committee, being clear about what you want

---

2. The Rev. Richard J. Kirk, Organizational Consultant for Congregations, developed this structure.

and do not want from each. Questions that need to be addressed include: the budget for each committee; the type of profile desired (website, printed, CD); how much to use computer technology for a paper-reduced process; the desired date for submission of candidates' names to the vestry; and the number of candidates' names desired. These items need to be communicated to the committees in a timely manner. Also, it is important to keep in close contact with your diocesan Transition Ministries Officer, especially at the beginning. The Discernment Process will vary in each diocese and she/he is the one who will guide you each step of the way. Meet with him/her first, before making any decisions.

It is best if each member of the vestry, Self-Study Committee, and Discernment Committee can read this book to gain a clear understanding of the process in which they are involved. In addition, *Discerning God's Will Together: A Spiritual Practice for the Church* by Danny E. Morris and Charles M. Olsen provides a cogent and concise discussion of discernment processes in congregations. Whether the decision-making revolves around choosing a new priest or another matter of importance in the congregation, both books will serve you well.

Last but by no means least, as soon as your two committees are chosen, set a time for the Discerning Your Gifts Retreat (see pages 13 to 21). It is best for this retreat to include all members of the vestry, Self-Study Committee, and Discernment Committee. It will set the tone for all that is to follow. Prior to candidate interviews, both the vestry and Discernment Committee should be guided through the Anti-Racism Workshop as well (see pages 60 to 70).

There is a magnificent journey ahead for each one of you as you lead your congregation during this time of transition. There is much to learn as you and your congregation work together to discern the will of God. May God richly bless you in the months ahead.

QUICK REFERENCE GUIDE

Discernment Process
(Search Process)

Discernment Committee
(Search Committee)

Self-Study Committee
(Profile Committee)

Transition Ministries Officer
(Deployment Officer)

Transition Consultant
(Search Consultant)

Conversation, Meeting, Mutual Discernment
(Interview)

PART ONE

BEGINNING
THE JOURNEY

◆ *Gifts for Transition*

If you are holding this book in your hands, most likely you are on the vestry, Self-Study Committee, or Discernment Committee of a congregation undergoing a change in clergy leadership. The future is a question mark, uncertainty looms, and you know that somehow you are in the role of giving shape and voice to that uncertainty, through the calling of your next rector or vicar—an awesome responsibility, one that will lay heavily on you at times, challenge you at others, and fill you with joy at still others.

You are beginning a new phase of your spiritual journey, a journey to which you have been called. The people in your congregation have seen something in you, some gift of the Holy Spirit, which has led them to either elect or appoint you to a special role in your church's Discernment Process. *As others have discerned the needed gifts in you, you are now called to discern the gifts needed in the next priest who will lead your congregation or to discern which candidate best embodies those gifts.*

As you begin this journey, it is helpful to be aware of your own particular gifts of the Spirit as well as of the reality that you are called to use those gifts during a time of transition, for your congregation and for yourself. How you personally deal with transition will necessarily affect your role in the Discernment Process. So first, let's talk a bit about transitions.

Simply living, being, and moving through the life cycle forces us into one transition after another. Just think of all the transitions you have been through. Transitions from home to nursery school, into the upper grades, then leaving home for college or a job. Transitions in changing jobs, moving from one community to another, saying good-bye to friends and familiar places, joining new churches. Transitions of getting married or partnered, children growing up and leaving home, losing loved ones to death, facing unexpected illness—and the list goes on.

As you begin this significant new role in the life of your parish, you may want to begin by reflecting on some of the transitions you have experienced. What were they? How did they affect you? What was it like for you and for those who love you? Were any of your transition periods accompanied by great emotionality? If so, how did you deal with it? Did your faith play a role? Your prayer life?

Knowing your own transition patterns will be helpful to you as you assume a leadership role during this time of transition in the life of your congregation. If you are not clear about your patterns or the role transition has previously played in your life, you might want to discuss this with another member of your committee, a trusted friend, a priest, or a spiritual director. Journaling can also be helpful in uncovering those feelings that may not be readily accessible to you. Whatever method works best for you, self-awareness of how you personally respond during times of uncertainty or loss will stand you in good stead as you begin this new phase of your spiritual journey.

If you are currently experiencing a major transition in your own life, you may want to discuss this with your priest, a trusted friend, or an advisor. Where are you in that process? Is it a particularly emotional one for you right now? If so, you may want to reevaluate your role in this process. How you feel about one transition in your life will affect how you feel and react to the ups and downs of the Discernment Process. It is important to focus on self-care and it begins now, so if this is not the right time for you to be engaged in this ministry, do not hesitate to say so at the beginning.

As I write this chapter it is the season after Pentecost, a time when we Christians focus on the Holy Spirit and all the many manifestations of her gifts and grace. For many people, both in the sacred and secular worlds, the early months of the season after Pentecost are a time of beginnings and endings. Traditionally, it is a time for graduation ceremonies and weddings, in which we both celebrate and let go of a life we have known and loved for many years. It is a time in which we might feel a sense of accomplishment and completion for what has gone before, along with butterflies in our stomach for what is yet to be. It is a time of letting go of the familiar when we cannot fully embrace the new because we have not yet experienced it. The new tomorrow that awaits us is fuzzy and filled with questions, because all the pieces are not yet in place.

My husband Michael and I are preparing to take our youngest child, Mike, to college next month. I know that things will never quite be the same again. I know that our family unit on a day-to-day basis will now be two rather than three. But I am also aware that I don't really know what this will mean for us as a couple, because we haven't experienced it yet. As a result, there is part of me that hasn't accepted, much less embraced, this new reality.

I realized this last week when Mike was staying over at a friend's house one night. As we turned out the downstairs lights, I reminded my husband to be sure to leave the outside light on for Mike when he came home. Then it hit me. He's not coming home tonight and in another month, he won't be coming home for months at a time. He'll be away at college. And I had my first jolt of reality about his leaving.

Our psyches have a way of protecting us in situations involving loss—whether it's the death of a loved one, or something very happy and exciting like a loved one leaving for college or entering a well-deserved retirement or accepting a new call. Our psyches protect us by letting the reality seep gradually into our souls. In all the grief situations I have been involved in either personally or with others, I don't believe there is one where the new reality hit full-force all at once. There has always been some denial going on simultaneously with the gradual acceptance and understanding of what the loss really means.

Just as children are meant to move on to college or a job some day, so priests are meant to answer another call or retire. It is part of the rhythm and movement of life and I believe that it is particularly part of the rhythm and movement of the Christian life. Why? Because in the final analysis, for all of us, whatever our situation, there is only one being who is eternal and permanent, and that is God. It is only God who is with us always to the close of the age and into eternity. It is only God who ultimately can fill that aching longing we have for the holy. It is only God who never leaves us, even for a moment.

Several years ago I was privileged to be the keynote speaker in the Diocese of Arkansas for a yearly event called the Women's Institute. It was held in a camp on the side of a mountain overlooking the most beautiful valley and mountains I have ever seen. In fact the "stained glass window" behind the altar, with a cross in the middle of it, was actually clear glass with a view of the incredible scope of God's creation.

On Saturday night it is their tradition to host an event called Cabin Fun, filled with imaginative and funny skits. One woman's skit was just to stand up and tell a story by herself. Like all good stories it began, "Once upon a time...." She then told the story of two little boys who were constantly in trouble at school and with their parents. They were brothers two years apart. They weren't delinquents; they were just full of mischief and liked to pull a lot of pranks that continually kept them in the principal's office. Finally, after a prank that went a little too far, in desperation their parents sent them to talk to their parish priest. They decided to send them in separately—the old divide-and-conquer routine—and they sent the youngest boy, who was around seven, in first.

The rector looked at him and said, "John, where is God?" John sat there in silence. So the rector raised his voice a little and said, "John, where is God?" The child sat there in stony silence. Finally, exasperated, the priest bellowed out, "Where is God?" The little boy's eyes got real big and suddenly he bolted out of the room.

He ran all the way home and immediately went upstairs and hid in his closet. His brother had been waiting for him to get home and ran after him upstairs, concerned that things had really gone wrong. "What happened, John? What'd that priest do to you?"

"Nothing yet," he said, shaking and trembling, "but they've lost God and they think we had something to do with it."

The good news is that God does not get lost, or graduate, or retire, or move. God has been in your church since before your church was conceived and God will be there until after the last bell has rung, if in fact that ever occurs. God is our alpha and omega, our beginning and our end. Focusing on the permanence of God throughout your Discernment Process for a new rector or vicar will ground you, the vestry or committee on which you serve, and the members of your congregation.

It is my prayer that this book will help you do just that. Let the journey begin!

Eternal God, in whom we live and move and have our being, you have been with me throughout all the transitions of my life. Be with me now as I seek to serve you by serving my congregation during our search for a priest to lead us. Help me to look honestly and without fear at other times of transition in my life and to deal with any unresolved issues related to them. Strengthen my desire to pray daily and my commitment to the task that lies ahead; in the name of the Source, the Word, and the Spirit. Amen.

Discerning Your Gifts Retreat

Now there are varieties of gifts, but the same Spirit; and there are varieties of services, but the same Lord. . . . (1 Cor. 12:4–5)

One of the most important aspects of the Discernment Process is the interaction between the vestry, the Self-Study Committee, and the Discernment Committee. When this relationship is healthy, open, and trusting the process can be seamless and life-giving to those involved. When it is not, frustration and burnout can occur, leading some people to question why they ever agreed to serve. In such circumstances, I have seen parishioners tender their resignation from the vestry or committee in the middle of the process. I have seen wardens and committee chairs resign. Such an outcome can be devastating and can derail the Discernment Process, which multiplies the sense of frustration, spreading it throughout the congregation.

A Discerning Your Gifts Retreat for vestry, Self-Study Committee, and Discernment Committee members together, at the very beginning of the Discernment Process, can establish a spiritual tone for all that is to follow, build a sense of teamwork among these three critical groups, and help members become aware of their own spiritual gifts as well as the gifts of those with whom they will be working. It can replace the annual vestry retreat to be sensitive to vestry members' time commitments. It can be held overnight in a retreat center, if money permits, or as a Friday night/Saturday retreat in a nearby church with participants sleeping at home. However you schedule it, the retreat should not be held in your own church facility. It is best to get away from all distractions and to view this as a sacred time apart from the normal routine of church work.

The Discerning Your Gifts Retreat included in this chapter can be led by anyone who is an experienced retreat or workshop leader—lay and clergy alike. Everything needed to lead it is here in the three sessions that follow. In Session 1, an additional two facilitators will be needed.

Session 1
REKINDLING YOUR LIGHT

MATERIALS NEEDED	Nametags, whiteboard and markers, meditative music, CD player, individual candles with drip holders for each participant, matches, "This Little Light of Mine" (160 or 221 in *Lift Every Voice and Sing II*)
HANDOUTS	Scripture Passages about Community
QUOTATION	"You are the light of the world." (Matt. 5:14)

1. Seat participants in groups of eight to ten, with a facilitator for each group. Each group should have its own whiteboard and marker.

2. The retreat leader gives the following talk or something similar to everyone:

> Each one of you here has been chosen—chosen to lead your congregation during the time of transition known as the Discernment Process. And you have said yes. You have stepped up and answered this call, not knowing exactly how much work it will entail or where the journey ultimately will lead you or your parish. You may be wondering, "Why me? What gifts do I bring?" Or if you're being honest, you may be thinking, "Why is she/he involved in this effort? What can that person contribute?" Or, "So-and-so drives me crazy. How can I work productively with him/her?" Right now, just know that there is a reason every one of you is here and that all the gifts needed are in this room.
>
> "This little light of mine, I'm going to let it shine." In the words of this familiar song lies a great truth, yet one that eludes many people throughout their life. Many people truly don't believe they have a light to shine. They look about them and feel that somehow their talents don't measure up, aren't worthy, aren't needed. So they keep their light to themselves, truly believing they have nothing to give.
>
> Yet in Matthew's gospel Jesus tells each one of us, "You are the light of the world" (5:14). Here Jesus is not speaking only to some who have been given special gifts or talents, but to everyone.
>
> What can we do if "this little light of mine" seems shrouded in darkness? First of all, we can remember that the light was never ours to begin with, but God's. In John's gospel Jesus tells us, "I am the light of the world. Whoever follows me will never walk in darkness but will have the light of life" (8:12). Jesus is *the* light and can become *our* light when we acknowledge the One who dwells within each one of us. The

light that shines within us and outside us is the light of Christ given to us at baptism.

What has happened to the light given to you at baptism? Has it flourished and grown brighter over the years in service to Christ? Has it all but disappeared, because you've forgotten it's there? Or is it a combination of the two? Sometimes you're a gleaming beacon of light for all to see and at other times you can't decide what light you have or where it's supposed to shine? Or, has your light burned out?

To be beacons of light in a world filled with darkness, we need to nurture and focus on the light within us. This retreat gives all of us a wonderful opportunity to focus on the special gifts God has given to us and to each other—gifts you have been given not only to complete your church's Discernment Process but to grow spiritually through it. This weekend we are all going to help one another discover the many lights, the many gifts that each one of us has within us, just waiting to be uncovered. As we focus on that light and discover new ways to share that light with others, we can come alive in Christ, not only as individuals, but also as a church. And we will realize that all the gifts needed for a productive Discernment Process are right here in this room.

To begin to look at the light that was given us at baptism, I'd like to talk for a moment about the meaning of baptism. The Book of Common Prayer tells us that "Holy Baptism is full initiation by water and the Holy Spirit into Christ's Body the Church. The bond which God establishes in Baptism is indissoluble" (BCP 298). So this covenant we have made with God is eternal. There's nothing we can do to get out of it. If we're baptized, we're baptized, and that's it. And in our baptism, we have all been made ministers. We are all ministers—and what is ministry? It's a whole new way of being, not just a way of doing.

To go into the ministry is not to be ordained, but to be baptized. Who are the ministers of your church? You are! Yes, you have clergy who serve your congregation, but *you* are the ministers. Throughout much of its history, the church has denied this scope of vocation to ministry and given higher credence and respect to clergy vocations. Today this church tradition is being guided back to an awareness of the breadth of vocation to ministry, notably in terms of its expression by the laity.

You all may have heard clergy saying they want to "empower the laity." But of this concept Stewart Zabriskie writes in his book *Total Ministry,* "I see this whole notion of 'empowering the laity' as being condescending to those who have been unable to do anything all along, which is far from the case. That same mindset has also retranslated the word *lay* to divert its roots in *laos* to a secondary and more popular sense of 'inexpert.'" He goes on to say that an essential part of understanding total ministry is to listen to those who are already ministering as Christ's body. "Listening is more important than devising systems to 'empower' the laity, those who are already expressing the Spirit's power."[1] Right now, I'd like us all to listen to ourselves and to each other in our small groups. *(Break into small groups at this time, and play appropriate music to help people get comfortable.)*

3. Small group facilitators state:

Think back to a moment in your childhood when you felt really cared for or when someone did something special for you. Name the caregiver and what she/he did, then share it with the group. *(Leader writes what each person says on whiteboard. When everyone has spoken, the leader marks through each caregiver's name and writes "Jesus," telling the person who shared, "Jesus did this for you.")*

Now I want you to think of a time in your life when you did something for someone else. *(Write answers on whiteboard.)* It's once again Jesus who did this for the other person, through you. You were sharing your gift of ministry with that other person.

4. Continue with large group discussion as follows:

In Colossians St. Paul tells Archippus, "See that you fulfil the ministry which you have received in the Lord" (4:17, RSV). Each one of you here has already done that to some extent. And why? Because ministry takes place:

1. Wherever a Christian happens to be.
2. Whenever a Christian is called to minister.
3. With whomever a Christian happens to meet.
4. Using whatever gifts a Christian has been given.[2]

Before we close, I'd like us to celebrate the light of Christ within each one of us by taking a candle and lighting one another's candles, saying as we do so, "The light of Christ." Then when all of our candles are lit, we'll sing together, "This little light of mine, I'm going to let it shine, let it shine, let it shine."

5. At the end of this session, give out copies of "Scripture Passages about Community" (page 21). Ask each participant to select one passage to meditate on throughout the retreat, saying:

Keep the passage close to your heart. Let the words enter your very being. Bring this handout with you to the last session.

1. Stewart G. Zabriskie, *Total Ministry: Reclaiming the Ministry of All God's People* (Bethesda, Md.: The Alban Institute, 1995), 10.

2. Patricia N. Page, *All God's People Are Ministers: Equipping Church Members for Ministry* (Minneapolis: Augsburg Fortress, 1993), 20.

Session 2
DISCERNING YOUR GIFTS

MATERIALS NEEDED   Paper and thin marker for each participant,
                      masking tape

QUOTATION   "Now there are varieties of gifts, but the same
                      Spirit; and there are varieties of services, but
                      the same Lord; and there are varieties of activi-
                      ties, but it is the same God who activates all of
                      them in everyone." (1 Cor. 12:4–6)

1. Begin with the following talk or something similar to everyone together:

In our last session, we talked about our vocation to ministry beginning with our baptism. Jesus' own baptism by John the Baptist in the Jordan River was the beginning of this new covenant between God and us. It was the beginning of Jesus' ministry, which continues through us, the covenant community. When you and I are baptized, we become part of this ministry of Jesus. We are grafted into the body of Christ. Paul told the Christians in Corinth, "Now you are the body of Christ and individually members of it" (1 Cor. 12:27).

What does it mean to be part of the body of Christ? It means a lot of things. One of the most poignant passages of scripture on this topic is when Paul tells us, "If one member suffers, all suffer together with it; if one member is honored, all rejoice together with it" (1 Cor. 12:26). It also means that we are all a different part of the same body. (Read aloud 1 Corinthians 12:14–26. Explain.)

Why is this a difficult concept to grasp sometimes? Because we've all been shaped by Western individualism that says, "I am my own person; I live for myself or my family alone; I rise and fall on my own merit." But Christianity is completely counter to this. Completely. If you don't take away anything from this retreat, please take away this. Being part of a Christian community means that we're never alone—or we don't have to be. We're all on a journey together. If one member suffers, everyone suffers with that person. If one member is honored, all rejoice. If we don't have a particular gift that is needed for ministry, someone else will. It means we're a *team* in the best sense of that word. Not in competition for the best spot, because there is no best spot. All the spots are equal.

The former bishop of the Episcopal Diocese of Nevada tells the story of a Palm Sunday a number of years ago. His family had just come home directly from church, and he and his wife were in the kitchen preparing lunch. Suddenly their kindergartner came in from outside, stood in the doorway, and announced, "I can tell you what the people said when Jesus rode into town on a donkey." He paused to make sure he had it just right, and said, "Hosanna, I'm the highest."[3]

Let's sing that together, beginning as the little boy did, and we'll add some more verses. Just repeat after me. "Hosanna, I'm the highest." *(Repeat.)* "Hosanna, I'm the lowest." *(Repeat.)* "Hosanna, it doesn't matter." *(Repeat.)*

And why not? Why doesn't it matter? *(Elicit responses from the group.)*

There does seem to be concern when we start talking about gifts for ministry about which gift is the best, which person is the highest—and this goes back to the time of St. Paul. This truly has nothing to do with what it means to be part of the body of Christ. Can we say that a hand is better than a foot, or a heart is better than a stomach? No, of course we can't.

We have all been given gifts of the Spirit at baptism, but there are varieties of gifts. An important question for every Christian is, "What particular gifts have been given to me through the Spirit and how can I use those gifts in the service of the Lord?" The question for each of you here today is a bit more specific. "What gifts have I been given that are needed during our Discernment Process and how am I meant to use them?"

In 1 Corinthians St. Paul tells us, "Now there are varieties of gifts, but the same Spirit; and there are varieties of services, but the same Lord; and there are varieties of activities, but it is the same God who activates all of them in everyone. To each is given the manifestation of the Spirit for the common good" (12:4–7). He goes on to state that the gifts of the Spirit include prophecy, administration, healing, preaching, discernment, and faith. In his letter to the Galatians Paul says, "the fruit of the Spirit is love, joy, peace, patience, kindness, generosity, faithfulness, gentleness, and self-control" (5:22–23).

What are your gifts and fruits of the Spirit? If you're like most people, you haven't really thought about it, or you may be certain you have some gifts and not others. But there's only one way to test out what we think, and that's in community. So here we are in community, and we're going to see if how we perceive our gifts is the way others perceive them.

2. Ask the participants to tape a piece of paper to their back and take a marker. Then ask them to write on the other participants' papers the gifts they perceive God has given to that person. When everyone has finished writing, ask them to remove their papers and read the gifts aloud.

---

3. Zabriskie, *Total Ministry,* 14.

3. Now read and talk about the following passage from Patricia Page's book *All God's People Are Ministers:*

> God has given and continues to give gifts to each person, and God does not want those gifts wasted. God's bounteous gifts stretch us as a community to find ways to use the gifts of each member in its mission. Paul was clear that the gifts were not given for individual use or glory. Rather, "to each is given the manifestation of the Spirit for the common good" (1 Cor. 12:7). The shape and mission of each Christian communion, in its local and wider gatherings, becomes reformed as each person with his or her unique gifts is incorporated into the body. The metaphor, *the gifted community,* also challenges us to delve deeper into the implications of being a community created by God for God's purposes, as a gift to the world (see Ephesians 1:3–14).[4]

3. Instruct participants to hold on to their list of gifts, as they will be using it in the next session. Between now and then instruct them to think about one of their gifts that they would like to write on their nametag to bring to the next session. Instruct them also to bring the handout "Scripture Passages about Community," which was given in the first session.

Session 3
USING YOUR GIFTS IN COMMUNITY

MATERIALS NEEDED	Meditative music; paper and pen for each participant; "This Little Light of Mine" (160 or 221 in *Lift Every Voice and Sing II*)
HANDOUTS	Scripture Passages about Community
QUOTATION	"To each is given the manifestation of the Spirit for the common good." (1 Cor. 12:7)

1. Play meditative music. Allow participants about one hour to meditate on their chosen scripture passage and the gift they have chosen to put on their nametag. Instruct them as follows:

> Repeat the scripture text over and over, eventually zeroing in on a few words or even a single word. Keep repeating the words that you distilled from your text. Let God touch you through the word or words. Let these holy words take root in your being. Then add your gift. Listen to God's word for you. How do you feel God means for you to use your gift during the Discernment Process? If helpful, put your thoughts on the

---

4. Page, *All God's People Are Ministers,* 19.

paper given to you. You'll have one hour for this exercise, so find a place where you can be comfortable.

2. When the participants have gathered again, ask them to share their findings with one other person, then with the group as a whole. Write everyone's gifts on whiteboard for all to see, stressing their interrelatedness, differences, and strengths. You may want to point out what gifts God has given to each committee as a whole and how the different committees can help and complement each other throughout the Discernment Process. Let participants know that as soon as the retreat is over, the role of each individual committee will be to pray for the committee that is engaged in the primary work at that time. For example, if the Self-Study Committee is involved in writing the profile/website, the vestry and Discernment Committee members should pray for that process and for individual committee members.

3. Ask participants to share any insights they may have received during the retreat, to ask questions, or to make comments.

4. Sing "This Little Light of Mine."

5. Encourage members of the Discernment Committee and vestry to do some foundational reading while the Self-Study Committee is working on the profile/website. *Discerning God's Will Together: A Spiritual Practice for the Church* by Danny E. Morris and Charles M. Olsen[5] is the best book I have found to help people begin to focus on what discernment is all about. Its five chapters are entitled simply "Discernment: What, Why? Who? How? Where?" The biblical foundation focuses on general decision-making in the church, not specifically on the Discernment Process leading to the calling of a rector or vicar. However, it provides a solid background for the meetings and reflections in this book that will help Discernment Committee members and vestry members as they seek to shape their process in accordance with Christian principles. All vestry and committee members should have their own copy of this book, enabling them to work on their personal spiritual development as the process unfolds.

6. End with a closing prayer by the group. Have participants stand in a circle with everyone holding hands. Each person is to thank God for the person next to him/her and for the gift(s) she/he brings to the Discernment Process. *(The gifts will be written on the nametags.)* The leader then sums up the many blessings God has given their church through the ministries and gifts offered to it by the group.

---

5. Danny E. Morris and Charles M. Olsen, *Discerning God's Will Together: A Spiritual Practice for the Church* (Bethesda, Md.: Alban Publications, 1997).

SCRIPTURE PASSAGES ABOUT COMMUNITY[6]

I, Yahweh, speak with directness. I express myself with clarity. Assemble, come, gather together...consult with each other. (Isaiah 45:19–21, JB)

Where two or three are gathered in my name, there am I in the midst of them. (Matthew 18:20, RSV)

Let us consider how to stir up one another to love and good works, not neglecting to meet together...but encouraging one another. (Hebrews 10:24–25, RSV)

If one member [of the body of Christ] suffers, all suffer together with it; if one member is honored, all rejoice together with it. (1 Corinthians 12:26, NRSV)

Now the whole group of those who believed were of one heart and soul. (Acts 4:32, NRSV)

Moses' father-in-law said to him, "What you are doing is not good. You will surely wear yourself out, both you and these people with you. For the task is too heavy for you; you cannot do it alone." (Exodus 18:17–18, NRSV)

The whole Body is fitted and joined together, every joint adding its own strength. (Ephesians 4:16, JB)

They called the church together and related all that God had done with them. (Acts 14:27, NRSV)

Now there are varieties of gifts, but the same Spirit....To each is given the manifestation of the Spirit for the common good. (1 Corinthians 12:4, 7, NRSV)

6. This handout may be downloaded from www.churchpublishing.org/callingclergy.

PART TWO

STARTING THE SELF-STUDY

◆ *Pre-Meeting Reflections*

The first gathering of the Self-Study Committee as a distinct group will lay the groundwork for all that is to follow. Before establishing a meeting date, contact the Transition Ministries Officer in your diocese to determine the expectations of your bishop with regard to this part of the Discernment Process. Most dioceses will have specific guidelines for you to follow. For example, some dioceses offer Transition or Search Consultants to walk with you through the Discernment Process. Often they are paid by the congregation; sometimes they are volunteers. Find out the procedure in your diocese. In addition, it is often a requirement that your Transition Ministries Officer approve the financial and other information in your profile before it is posted on your website, published in booklet format, or sent to the Church Deployment Office (CDO) of the Episcopal Church in New York. Before any meeting dates are established, make sure you are aware of the resources offered as well as the requirements expected by your diocesan office.

Next, make certain you communicate with your wardens. Are there any mandates or guidelines from them? *Remember, you serve on a subcommittee of the vestry; guidance from them at the outset is critical to avoiding problems later on.*

For example, does your vestry want you to produce a booklet profile or a website profile? What does your Transition Ministries Officer suggest? Many churches are now using their websites to post information that candidates will need to acquaint them with their church. This approach makes both economic and evangelistic sense. A tremendous amount of time, energy, and money is involved in producing a quality profile. Unfortunately, if it is in booklet format only it will have a very narrow, limited use. Candidates and church members will read it once and that is usually all, regardless of how compelling and professional a product it is.

The incredible work, prayer, and commitment that go into producing your parish profile should be shared with as wide an audience as possible. Since seekers and newcomers often use the Internet to find a church, why not use the same time commitment to produce something that is lasting and attracts new members to your church, as well as attracts potential candidates? In addition, the cost of a glossy color booklet can be quite high. Why not use the Internet for an attractive, catchy presentation of your congregation? Before your first meeting, make sure you have a vestry decision on this or are clear that they have relegated the decision to the Self-Study Committee.

The most important task you will have is choosing a Spiritual Guide for your committee. Who on your committee immediately comes to mind as a person of prayer? Whose spiritual insight might you seek in a time of need? Begin praying for the guidance of the Holy Spirit regarding this selection. Resource 1 offers special guidance to your Spiritual Guide as she/he assumes this role with your committee.

> *Most loving God, be with our committee as we begin the task you have set before us. Give us discerning hearts as we choose a Spiritual Guide for our group to shepherd us throughout this process. O blessed Creator, you created each one of us with unique gifts and talents. Help me to appreciate mine and not hide them under a bushel, as I appreciate the many gifts you have given to those with whom I will serve; in the name of the Triune God. Amen.*

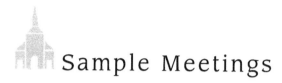

Sample Meetings

◆ *First Self-Study Committee Task Cluster*

PRIMARY GOALS   Team Building
                       Outline of Tasks, End Results

From these sample meetings, pick and choose what will work best for your group. Be sure to contact your diocesan Transition Ministries Officer before you meet as she/he will have additional information for you, related to your particular diocesan process. Regular communication with your diocesan office will save your committee valuable time.

I. Continue the prayerful tone established on retreat. Begin with prayer and choose a Spiritual Guide as your first task. Who among you has been given special gifts of prayer and discernment? Whom do you trust to guide you in discerning the will of the Holy Spirit? Discuss as a group and reach a decision, praying for the guidance of the Holy Spirit.

Your Spiritual Guide can use one of the prayer methods discussed in Resource 1 at each meeting. For this gathering, pass around a special object like a rock, cross, prayer beads, symbol of your church, or any religious object. The person holding it prays silently for about five minutes, while the meeting is in session. She/he then passes it to the next person, who begins praying silently. Continue until the meeting ends.

II. Team building[1]
   a. What are your expectations as our work begins? What are your hopes and fears?
   b. What was your spiritual gift discerned at the retreat? How do you see yourself using it on this committee?

III. Develop group norms, such as: pray creatively throughout the meetings; pray daily for committee members and their work; begin

---

1. McGraw-Hill publishes several excellent books for team building and group mixers: *Team Games for Trainers, More Games Teams Play, Even More Games Trainers Play,* and *201 Icebreakers.*

and end all meetings on time; attend all meetings unless chairperson is called in advance; significantly reduce the amount of paper used; complete all assigned tasks on time; maintain confidentiality; communicate openly and honestly; listen with understanding; do not monopolize or force one's opinion.

IV. Discuss the people who are here to serve as resources for you:

> *It is best to state at the outset that no interim clergy, present staff, or consultant may become a candidate for rector or vicar in your particular congregation. The entire congregation should be notified of this in the first communication from the Self-Study Committee.*

a. Your diocesan Transition Ministries Officer.

b. Your Transition Consultant, if you have one. Your consultant can: 1) explain how she/he came to be with you and the role of a consultant in the group; 2) explore your expectations of the consultant and clarify if necessary.

V. Note the tasks before you:

a. *Choosing a recording secretary.* Display minutes of the Self-Study meetings in a prominent place.

b. *Communicating to the parish and diocese.* The importance of regular communication with your vestry, congregation, and diocesan office cannot be overstated. Choose a person to coordinate all communication. (See "Mountain Climber Poster," Resource 7.) The committee might also want to set up a Self-Study Committee bulletin board.

c. *Maintaining confidentiality.* At this point in the process almost nothing is confidential because nothing about the "process" is confidential. However, when the Discernment Committee receives names, all names of interested clergy are to be treated with the utmost confidentiality. A name, not process, is the issue with confidentiality.

d. *Discussing the difficult issues* that exist in most congregations and not being afraid to name them in the profile. Honesty and transparency in the profile are critical to a successful Discernment Process.

e. *Creating a profile* in two formats:

- • List primary parts of the profile:
    1. Mission Statement and Goals.
    2. Key Statistics: Average Sunday Attendance (ASA).
    3. Programs and Organizations.
    4. Financial Summary (be brief; avoid complex tables).
    5. Distinctive Features: cluster or other collaborative arrangements, facilities, school.
    6. History of the Congregation (be brief; include both blessings and challenges).

7. Information on Diocese and Community.
8. Hopes and Dreams of Members.
9. Qualities Sought in a New Priest.[2]
- Gather data from the survey provided in Resource 9,[3] focus group meetings, town hall meeting, interviewing committee chairs.
- Collate gathered data.
- Prioritize and process data.
- Create two profiles:
    1. A website,[4] print, CD, and/or video profile for candidates.
    2. A computer profile for the Episcopal Church deployment office, downloadable from www.episcopalchurch.org/cdo as Parish Search Request Form.

f. *Enjoying a sense of humor!* Share Resource 8 whenever members could use a good laugh.

VI. Create an Action Plan with timeline. Be sure to have commitments at this meeting to deal with the work that can be done early, such as financial data, worship data, and parish statistics. In addition, you will need:
- A person with computer skills for data processing.
- A person or people who are skilled in writing.
- Someone to collate and distribute surveys. The sample survey in Resource 9 can be given to this volunteer to look over and make recommendations at the next meeting.
- A lead person to put the focus groups together and coordinate the format, dates, and times for focus group gatherings.
- People who are good focus group facilitators.
- A person to take the newsprint notes from the focus group meetings and type them for the committee, unless a computer is utilized at the meeting.

VII. At the end of the meeting, ask members what it was like for them to pray during the meeting while holding the object that was passed around. End with prayer.

---

2. Adapted from a PowerPoint presentation by the Diocese of Spokane.
3. As of the writing of this book, the Episcopal Church Center Deployment Office is piloting a survey called the Church Assessment Tool. Check with your diocesan Transition Ministries Officer on the status of this ground-breaking project and any costs that may be associated with using it.
4. A current Google search of the words "Episcopal parish profiles" produces 308,000 results. Many churches are therefore using this method of spreading the word about their congregation. To increase the chances of your profile receiving an Internet "hit," go to Google's "Webmaster Guidelines." This will tell your webster how to make your profile fit the Google search engines. (Taken from a presentation by the Rev. Canon Mark Gatza, Deployment Officer in the Diocese of Maryland.)

◆ Second Self-Study Committee Task Cluster

PRIMARY GOALS   Complete Survey
                       Review Action Plan

Your Spiritual Guide begins by discussing the type of prayer to be used during the meeting, as described in Resource 1.

I. The person responsible for studying the survey found in Resource 9, or others provided by your diocese or the Episcopal Church Center, presents his or her recommendations to the group. At this time a thorough discussion of the questions needs to take place among committee members. It may take more than one meeting to do this. Your Transition Consultant does not need to be present for all these meetings. However, it is best if this person approves the final product. Some churches have found it helpful to have the household questions in a different color, since only one family member is to fill out this section.

If written surveys are utilized, it is best to personally hand them out and collect them, rather than mail them. It takes more time but is worth the effort. Some churches distribute them during a worship service and provide time during the service for people to fill them out. (Mailings often do not generate a good rate of return and those with complaints are sometimes more likely to fill them out, skewing the data collected.)

An alternative to written questionnaires is to post your survey on an interactive website such as surveymonkey.com. For a fee, the survey is administered, tabulated, and the percent of return given. If your church has its own interactive website, your survey can of course be posted there.

A different methodology is used in the Diocese of East Carolina. Their survey is taken at the beginning of the focus group meetings and then serves as a starting point for discussion.

II. Review and update Action Plan and timeline.

Your Spiritual Guide closes the meeting.

Reflecting on the Process

Now that you have had several meetings, how are you feeling about serving on the Self-Study Committee? Is it what you thought it would be? How is it the same? How is it different?

Keeping in mind that your service is one of your primary lay ministries at this time, how are you using your spiritual gifts? Do you see opportunities to develop them further and to grow spiritually through this experience?

Are committee members being honest with one another about the real issues facing your congregation, or is there something unspoken in the room? If so, do you feel you might bring it up or discuss it with the chair of the committee?

You may find yourself beginning to lose your commitment to daily prayer as the work begins to intensify. Try to remain steadfast in your prayer for all members of your committee, for your vestry, your church, your Transition Consultant, your Transition Ministries Officer, your bishop. Pray also for all those priests, as yet unnamed, who will read your profile to discern a possible fit for them.

If you are gaining new spiritual insights into yourself, God, or the church, you might want to discuss them with your priest. She or he will most likely be delighted to sit down with you to discuss your spiritual progress or where you feel you would like to be growing. When I served in parish ministry, it truly made my day, if not my week, when a questioning, seeking parishioner sought me out for spiritual guidance. You might be surprised at how much more often priests are sought out for concerns about the broken heating system or the need for additional funds in the church budget. Working with someone on his/her spiritual growth is like manna from heaven for us. Indulge us a bit!

As you read that last paragraph, you may have found yourself thinking, That may be true, but she doesn't know my priest! If that's the case, or if you wish your interim had left the church yesterday, you might step out in faith and approach this person on a different level than you have before. So often our relationship with our clergy is based more on incidentals than on the deeper spiritual questions of life. Try it once! You might be surprised. If that is still not working for you, and you are serious about working on spiritual issues, ask for a referral to a nearby trained spiritual director.

Steadfast and searching God, continue to strengthen me for the journey ahead. Be with me as I look honestly at my church, my own role in its history, and my possible role in its future. Help me to hear your still, small voice for me personally, as I continue this work for the greater good. Where do you want me to grow? What do you want me to learn? Speak to me, God, I am listening. In the name of the Father, and of the Son, and of the Holy Spirit. Amen.

More Sample Meetings

♦ *Third Self-Study Committee Task Cluster*

PRIMARY GOALS   Focus Group Creation and Training
                       Committee and Community Interviewing
                       Action Plan Review

Before the next three task clusters are planned, be sure to contact your Transition Consultant or diocesan Transition Ministries Officer for information on how your diocese wishes you to proceed. Maintaining clear communication with your diocesan office is necessary for the smooth functioning of your process.

Your Spiritual Guide begins the gatherings.

I. Face-to-face meetings with parishioners and people in your community are important to the production of a good profile. Not only do focus groups with parishioners and church committees gather essential data, they also enable parishioners to feel they have had a voice in the Discernment Process. In addition, they require a commitment from a broad range of people. This is significant not only in terms of process, but also output.

   Make sure newcomers are invited to participate. Don't forget to include homebound parishioners and youth sixteen years of age and older as well. These groups are often overlooked when focus groups are being formed. In addition, a modified focus group process can be used with students in your church school. You may be surprised at their insight!

II. Before convening your focus groups, discuss as a committee the impact of your church's size on the clergy leader best suited for your congregation. In general, congregations are considered family size with an Average Sunday Attendance (ASA) of 50 or less; pastoral size, 50 to 150 ASA; transition size, nearing or slightly over 150 ASA; program size, 150 to 350 ASA; resource size, over 350 ASA. The skills needed in your priest will be different in each category.

Alban Institute research tells us that family-size congregations function best when they call a priest who will stay with them a long time. Bi-vocational clergy who are part time in the parish and part time in another vocation work well in this setting. Pastoral-size congregations need clergy with strong pastoral and interpersonal skills, as these congregations will be very priest-centered. Transition-size congregations are in a special category. It is very difficult to move from pastoral to program size; therefore a leader with specific skills is needed here. Someone who can lead a congregation through change, can manage change related to growth, and who has experience in congregational development is called for. In a program-size congregation there are numerous programs, many run by lay ministers. The rector/vicar cannot be involved in all of them. This pastor needs to be able to encourage lay ministry initiatives, to equip the saints. A resource-size congregation functions best with a priest with administrative skills who can manage a large staff, work well with diverse people, and exhibit excellence in preaching and leading worship.[5] Keeping these factors in mind when reviewing data received from focus groups and questionnaires will help you as you frame your profile and describe the cluster of gifts needed in your next rector or vicar.

It is also helpful to be aware of recent studies by Dr. Diana Butler Bass. Her study of fifty vital congregations found three common elements among them: 1) a focus on tradition as fluid (retraditioning); 2) a focus on spirituality as pilgrimage, as well as Christian community through hospitality, healing, social justice; and 3) a focus on an energizing goal.[6] Discussing the attributes of vital congregations can help your church look at areas of potential growth.

III. In convening the focus groups and writing your profile, build on your strengths as a congregation. Some churches tend to focus on what is wrong with their parish and needs to be "fixed." Instead, focus on what excites you most about your congregation, what energizes you, what you do well.

What you focus on becomes your reality. Focus on your strengths. This does not mean to ignore or minimize significant issues in your congregation. Be upfront and transparent in your profile about such issues. What is being suggested here is that you not concentrate on those issues in the focus group meetings and profile, but instead, focus on your strengths.

5. Roy M. Oswald, James M. Heath, and Ann W. Heath, *Beginning Ministry Together: The Alban Handbook for Clergy Transitions* (Washington, D.C.: The Alban Institute, 2003), 31.
6. See Diana Butler Bass, *Christianity for the Rest of Us: How the Neighborhood Church Is Transforming the Faith* (New York: Harper Collins, 2006) and Diana Butler Bass, *The Practicing Congregation: Imagining a New Old Church* (Virginia: The Alban Institute, 2004).

IV. Meet with parishioners in Focus Group Meetings. To train focus group leaders follow the guidelines in Resources 2 and 3.

V. Meet each committee in the church and ask the following or similar questions:
- Does your committee have an energizing goal? If so, what is it?
- What are your strengths?
- What do you need to build on those strengths?
- What help is needed from the new rector/vicar?

If time is an issue, the Self-Study Committee may want to give these questions to each committee chair for written feedback.

VI. Interview community leaders, such as your mayor, city council members, school principals, social service agencies, other churches. How can your church better serve your community? What are the needs of people in your community who are not part of any faith group? In searching for a new rector or vicar, do you want to consider someone with the qualities to reach out to those in your community outside your church? If not, why not?

Your Spiritual Guide closes these gatherings.

NOTE

Focus group meetings can be completed within six weeks. When all surveys are back, focus groups have completed their work, other interviews have been conducted, and data on worship, finances, and parish statistics is together, volunteers for the Action Plan can put the information into a form for the Self-Study Committee to evaluate. At that point, the committee can begin to write the profile, either in website, CD, or booklet form. I recommend, as stated earlier, not using a booklet format due to the cost of printing an attractive, colorful booklet. St. Mary Magdalene Episcopal Church in Maineville, Ohio, printed an attractive ledger-size, one-page, trifold document highlighting who they are as a congregation and focusing on their core values. A letter to prospective candidates was placed in the center of the document, along with a CD containing their profile. This same document is used for newcomers, with a different letter inserted. Now that's stewardship!

◆ Fourth Self-Study Committee Task Cluster

PRIMARY GOALS   Biblical Reflection
                         Completion of Written Parish Profile in Booklet
                            or Website Form
                         Action Plan Update

Completion of the written profile can be extremely time consuming if tasks are not shared equally by committee members and there is not a mechanism in place for pulling the material together. The most burned-out people I encounter are those who end up writing the profile singlehandedly. Such parishioners can end up disillusioned, frustrated, and angry that others are not carrying their weight. The beginning of this task cluster is a good time for a check-in with committee members.

Begin with your Spiritual Guide sharing the type of prayer to be used at this gathering and then move to a time of sharing.

I. Ask the members to describe in one word how they feel about the self-study process at this time.

II. Print the passage below from Mark 6:30–44 for each committee member. Have someone read it aloud. Ask members what phrase jumps out at them. Have someone else read it aloud. Ask members what word they hear for the Self-Study Committee in this passage. Discuss. Read aloud again and ask members what they hear God calling them to do through the words of the passage. Discuss. Close with prayer.

III. Discuss in detail the task assignments needed to finalize the writing of your written profile. Break into working committees if necessary. Remember, build on your strengths!

MARK 6:30-44

The apostles then rendezvoused with Jesus and reported on all that they had done and taught. Jesus said, "Come off by your-selves; let's take a break and get a little rest." For there was con-stant coming and going. They didn't even have time to eat.

So they got in the boat and went off to a remote place by themselves. Someone saw them going and the word got around. From the surrounding towns people went out on foot, running, and got there ahead of them. When Jesus arrived, he saw this huge crowd. At the sight of them, his heart broke—like sheep with no shepherd they were. He went right to work teaching them.

When his disciples thought this had gone on long enough—it was now quite late in the day—they interrupted: "We are a long way out in the country, and it's very late. Pronounce a benediction and send these folks off so they can get some supper.

Jesus said, "You do it. Fix supper for them."

They replied, "Are you serious? You want us to go spend a for-tune on food for their supper?"

But he was quite serious. "How many loaves of bread do you have? Take an inventory."

That didn't take long. "Five," they said, "plus two fish." Jesus got them all to sit down in groups of fifty or a hundred—they looked like a patchwork quilt of wildflowers spread out on the green grass! He took the five loaves and two fish, lifted his face to heaven in prayer, blessed, broke, and gave the bread to the disci-ples, and the disciples in turn gave it to the people. He did the same with the fish. They all ate their fill. The disciples gathered twelve baskets of leftovers. More than five thousand were at the supper.[7]

7. Eugene Peterson, *The Message: The Bible in Contemporary Language* (Colorado Springs: Navpress, 2002), 1820–1821.

◆ Fifth Self-Study Committee Task Cluster

PRIMARY GOAL   Completion of Parish/Institution Search
                      Request Form for Church Deployment Office

The Parish/Institution Search Request Form should be filled out by your Transition Consultant or your diocesan Transition Ministries Officer. It can be frustrating to try to fill this out on your own. I do not recommend spending your time in this way. Headaches often follow with little progress!

Your Spiritual Guide opens the meeting.

I. In approximately fifty words, describe your congregation as it is now. It must fit in the lines provided on the form that can be downloaded from www.episcopalchurch.org/cdo. If desired, break into two or three small groups to develop several rough drafts of a statement, then let your diocesan representative write them into a final statement at a later time. (See Resource 10, "Sample Congregational Statements.")

II. Write four primary goals for your congregation. With all the data that has been generated to this point, it should not be difficult to choose four primary areas for your congregation to focus on with a new priest. Look at the context of these goals in the parish computer profile. Each needs to be short enough to fit in the space provided, approximately ten words or less. Questions can flow naturally, or the SPACEPOW categories in Resource 11 can be a helpful tool.

III. Write four *related* responsibilities for the Responsibilities: Skills/Experience/Pastoral Specialties section of the form.

IV. Discuss the last line on the first page of the Parish/Institution Search Request Form that states: "Applications from Women and Minorities Especially Welcome." The minorities referred to here are racial minorities. When this box is checked, the Church Deployment Office will conduct an additional computer search, if necessary, to ensure that a balanced number of female and minority candidates are included. Your vestry and Discernment Committee members will be taking an Anti-Racism Workshop to help focus their attention on these issues.

V. Notify your parish priest that it is time to publicly thank the Self-Study Committee and then to commission the Discernment Committee. (See Resource 6.)

VI. Establish a time for the committee to have a celebration dinner together after members have read the reflection in the next chapter, "Passing the Baton."

Your Spiritual Guide closes this final meeting of the Self-Study Committee.

NOTE TO DIOCESAN TRANSITION MINISTRIES OFFICERS

1. Once the profile has reached this point, you or the Transition Consultant prepares the Parish/Institution Search Request Form. Most Self-Study Committees will need hands-on assistance here.

2. Choose pastoral specialties codes that highlight the responsibilities chosen by the committee. The more specific the codes, the better the chance of obtaining the right match for the congregation. Remember, the ministry statement, goals, responsibilities, and ministry specialties all need to be coordinated to create one complete picture of the congregation.

3. Be sure to review all financial information provided and check it against the parish's parochial report. If changes need to be made, the material then goes back to the Self-Study Committee and vestry for final approval.

4. When approval is obtained, the form can be faxed to the Church Deployment Office (CDO) in New York.

5. Several days later, CDO profiles of suitable candidates for the parish will be emailed to you. Make sure parish Discernment Committees know what procedure you will follow at this point, since processes vary widely from diocese to diocese. The particular process you choose to follow is less important than making sure you communicate that process consistently and widely with your congregation.

Passing the Baton

I always watch the summer Olympics with fascination. The divers and gymnasts inspire me to attempt to be graceful. The swimmers remind me of when I swam the butterfly for the twelve-and-unders with my local swim club. But it's the track stars who really capture my attention. I will admit here for the first time that I have never been able to run a complete mile without stopping. I do not know if the reason for this is psychological, physical, or a combination of both, but it has never happened. At the age of fifty-three it is probably not going to happen, but of course, I will not admit that—even to myself.

Nonetheless there was one track event at which I excelled as a child: running the relay. People who cannot run long distances—even one mile—can sometimes sprint rather quickly. So a sprinter I was, and I inevitably ended up on the relay team. The tricky part of running the relay was making a smooth transition, passing the baton to the next person so she/he could pick up where I left off.

This is what you are called to do now. Pass the baton. Your work as a member of the Self-Study or Discernment Committee is now over. What's happened has happened; what has not happened has not happened and it probably won't. Let it go. You've done your best. If you feel you have not given it all you could, be gentle with yourself. You probably gave what you could at the time, given the other factors in your life. This was not your only life commitment!

As you come to the end of this particular lay ministry to which you were called, I invite you to reflect back over the process in which you have been involved. What role did you play? What spiritual gifts did you use? How did you depend on your other committee members? You might want to give thanks for each of them and the gifts they brought to the endeavor. Give thanks to God for the gifts you were able to offer as well and for any insights gained.

If working on the Self-Study or Discernment Committee was not a pleasant experience for you, share those feelings with someone, perhaps your parish priest if you are comfortable doing so. What can you learn from this experience? What do you need to do to move beyond it?

After you have spent the amount of time you need in reflection and prayer, pass your baton. Some people find this to be more difficult than they thought. Others wish they had been able to pass it months ago! Wherever you find yourself, now is the time.

So go ahead. Pass the baton. You might find it helpful to imagine yourself passing it to one member of the Discernment Committee or vestry in particular. Pray for this person. Pray for his or her highest good and for his or her upcoming work on behalf of your congregation. Pray for the Discernment Committee or vestry as a whole, and once again, for each priest who will pray and discern if maybe, just maybe, your church is where God is calling him/her to serve.

> *Comforting God, you know my needs before I ask. Be with me in yet another transition, this time from serving in an active role in our Discernment Process to serving in a more passive one. Help me be content to rest a bit now and take pride in the work I have done. Let me not rush about like Martha, but like Mary, help me to sit at your feet to listen and learn. Guide me as I seek to discern your will for my ministry in the days ahead. In the name of your Child, our Savior, Jesus Christ. Amen.*

PART THREE

STARTING THE DISCERNMENT PROCESS

◆ Pre-Meeting Reflections

Please read the chapter "Beginning the Journey" in this book if you have not already done so. You are in the midst of transition, perhaps on several levels, and it is important to take this seriously. My hope is that you will read the Introduction and "Beginning the Journey" before you begin to digest the additional material contained in this chapter.

How you personally feel at the end of the Discernment Process, regardless of the outcome, will be determined in large part by the knowledge you have at the beginning, your ability to listen and learn from those who have been through many parish discernment processes (your diocesan representatives), your willingness to work in harmony with your wardens and vestry, your ability to work as a team with other members of your committee, and most importantly, the extent to which you view this as a ministry of discernment. My hope is you have had a chance to read *Discerning God's Will Together: A Spiritual Practice for the Church,* as suggested in the Discerning Your Gifts Retreat. This book will serve as an excellent spiritual foundation for your work in the months ahead.

It is helpful to be aware of several realities before you begin. First, this is not a brief commitment of your time. One person shared, "I wish I had known how long a process it would be. My only experience with hiring people was in the corporate world, where you fill a spot in three months." Most parish discernment processes take much longer than that unless you are conducting an abbreviated search with a short list of names without utilizing a parish profile. (This method sometimes

occurs in very small congregations with small budgets. Check with
your diocesan Transition Ministries Officer.)

Second, forget everything you learned about hiring in the secular
world. Your vestry is not *hiring* anyone; they are *calling* someone to a
ministry, which is radically different not only in content, but in process.
Your role is *discerning* the best person or people for the vestry to call,
not suggesting whom they should hire.

Throughout this book, I will refer to your committee as a
Discernment Committee, rather than a Search Committee. Why?
Because at the heart of each and every decision you make will be the
willingness to take the time to discern God's will for your church, then
the resolve to act on that will when you discern it. A Discernment
Process rooted in scripture and the tradition of our church, rather than
in psychological or business models, will lead you to a selection of
candidates based on the movement of the Holy Spirit in your midst.
There is a vast difference between this type of process and one that is
task-oriented or driven by an agenda or ego.

Third, trust the process outlined for you by your diocese. It will be
based on the wisdom of countless search and discernment processes
in the Episcopal Church. I have seen searches derailed when committees take the process into their own hands and proceed in a different
direction. Why does this happen? Because clergy expect certain standards in the church Discernment Process and gifted clergy will often
have a choice of churches. Unexpected behaviors and processes by a
particular Discernment Committee may send a signal to the clergyper-
son you do not want to send or are not even aware you are sending.

Maureen Frydlewicz, a Discernment Committee member from
Trinity Church in Cranford, New Jersey, wrote: "I wish I had understood
better how the diocese can be tapped early on for direction. I think I
thought of the diocese as being controlling, which was the wrong
assumption to make. I'm not sure why I felt that way, but during the
process I realized how helpful the diocesan leadership was."

Fourth, the Discernment Process for a rector or vicar can be filled
with times of jubilation and transformation, as well as disappointment
and sadness. Discernment Committee members sometimes feel like
they are on an emotional roller coaster ride. Ms. Frydlewicz stated further, "I think I went through every conceivable emotion—feeling over-
whelmed by the sense of responsibility, trying to keep an open mind in
the face of major disagreements, trying to be sure that the alpha per-
sonalities were listening to others, being impressed by the candidates'
resumes and not the candidate and vice versa, feeling up then down
over both good and bad meetings with candidates, wanting to keep
everything moving forward yet not wanting to rush the choice for fear

of making a mistake, wondering if our first choice would accept our call, and then, finally, just being so glad we had a new priest." This is a very common experience among members of Discernment Committees, which is why keeping yourself grounded in daily prayer is so important, not only to the process itself but for your own personal well-being.

Many church members, as well as committee members, feel anxiety during the Discernment Process for a new rector or vicar. Faithful prayer and communication among all parties involved will help diffuse this feeling, which is pervasive in parishes during a time of transition.

As your process unfolds, it is also helpful to expect the unexpected. One Discernment Committee chair stated, "When the candidate we unanimously voted to send to the vestry accepted another call, we felt like we had been jilted. We knew it was a fit. Why didn't she?" It is best to expect some moments of struggle as you and the candidates diligently work together to discern a possible call. Being aware at the outset that this is a process of *mutual* discernment between your committee and the priest is helpful in this regard.

Fifth, expect to be influenced by the activity of the Holy Spirit. This means that the process may not always go exactly as planned. It is important to remain flexible as you listen for the Spirit's movement among your group.

Finally, be vigilant in prayer. Kathy O'Hagan of St. Mark's and All Saints in Galloway, New Jersey, wrote, "I prayed all the time—for myself, team members, potential candidates, the parish. It seemed the more I prayed, the more people I found to pray for in the process! I knew the final choice was the correct one when I first spoke with the candidate. The team members weren't all there with me, as they were leaning toward the resume of someone else who never responded. I just let it roll as it should, as I knew it was in God's hands."

A focus at every meeting on listening to the Holy Spirit and mutually discerning a call will transform your process. The sample meetings and spiritual reflections in the pages that follow are designed to help you do that. In addition, daily prayer for your congregation, your vestry, your committee, and each candidate who comes before you will center you throughout this process, which can be grace-filled and life-giving. My prayer is that yours will be, with God's help.

Everlasting God of infinite power and goodness, you guided the Israelites as a pillar of fire: Guide me now as I seek to fulfill my responsibilities as a member of the Discernment Committee. Set my heart on fire with desire for you and your will only. Keep me from all that would distract me from hearing your voice and discerning your will for my congregation, as I participate in mutual discernment with our candidates in the days and months ahead. Show me, Lord; guide me; lead me. I need your help. Amen.

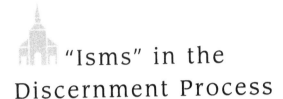 "Isms" in the Discernment Process

Yes, even in the year 2007, a separate chapter is called for to address the issue of the many "isms" that can come into play during a Discernment Process for the rector or vicar of a congregation. While many caring Christians today would declare themselves to be free from the biases of sexism, racism, and ageism, Episcopal Church statistics support the statement that these "isms" are still a factor in the Discernment Process.

This institutional problem is addressed by the Church Deployment Board of the Episcopal Church Center in the following stated policy:

> The policy established by the Board for Church Deployment is to search the CDO files without regard to race, marital status, age or sex, except to further by positive action the deployment of women and minorities. To that end, the CDO will ensure that search results include representative numbers of women and minorities.

At this time, the Church Deployment Office includes in their list of forty candidates for each search 20 percent who are women (or eight candidates), and 10 percent who are minorities (or four candidates). If the initial list of candidates produced by the computer search does not have these percentages, the system will automatically seed the list with the representative numbers. In addition, the CDO has been proactively promoting Latino clergy and supporting the placement of Asian clergy.[1]

While progress is being made, providing a balanced list of candidates has not resulted in balanced calls to date. In the report "The State of the Clergy 2006" by the Church Pension Group, Matthew J. Price, Ph.D., cites many current trends regarding the placement of clergy in the Episcopal Church today. Among his general findings are the following:

1. The career paths of clergywomen appear to differ significantly from those of clergymen.

1. Email from Pamela Ramsden, Associate Director, Church Deployment Officer, November 2, 2006.

2. For all active clergy, there is a persistent gap in compensation between men and women even when adjusting for position within the parish and years of credited service.

3. Age is a more important variable than gender in determining the probability that an ordinand (one newly ordained) will be employed in the church.

The male/female differences are significant. Newly ordained males are twice as likely to be employed as solo rectors as newly ordained females. Of all full-time clergy in the Episcopal Church, 71.3 percent are male; 28.7 percent are female. Nonetheless, 85.6 percent of senior rectors (in charge of a multi-clergy congregation) are male, while 14.4 percent are female. In addition, "when women are in sole clergy positions, they are in charge of congregations with lower Average Sunday Attendance (ASA) and Operating Revenues than is the case with male clergy and this is true regardless of years of Credited Service."[2]

Thirty years after the ordination of women to the priesthood, women clergy still seek parity in the church. And what about clergy of color? Today, in the Episcopal Church there are only two cathedral deans of color—in the Diocese of New Jersey and the Diocese of Newark. With approximately one hundred cathedrals in the Episcopal Church, that's only 2 percent. With Episcopal congregations still overwhelmingly Caucasian in makeup, for clerics of color to achieve parity they must receive calls from congregations that are predominately white.

The Diocese of New Jersey has had a budget of $40,000 or more for anti-racism training for the last eight years, doing without many other necessities to achieve this budget level. As an outgrowth of this effort, Discernment Committees are now required to have anti-racism training before meeting with potential candidates. In the last two years this has resulted in the calls of six clergy of color to predominately Caucasian congregations: four African Americans (which includes African and Caribbean clergy), one Hispanic, and one Indian (subcontinent). Out of 163 congregations, this represents only 3.7 percent of our churches, but most have not undergone searches in the last three years when the training has been required. This statistic is far from what we hope to achieve, but it is a start.

I include here a sampling of comments from other dioceses regarding the calling of clergy of color to predominately white congregations. At this time, there is not a comprehensive statistical analysis available; thus I conducted my own survey of all deployment officers in the Episcopal Church. The survey was not scientific and I received responses from some dioceses and not others. Nonetheless, the responses can be instructive.

2. Matthew J. Price, "The State of the Clergy 2006" (New York: Church Pension Group, 2006), 2, 10, 13.

Canon Jill Mathis writes: "We have 153 congregations in the Diocese of Pennsylvania. Only two predominately white congregations have called a priest of color."

The Rev. Canon Mark Gatza responded: "Currently we have no persons of color serving as rector or vicar of predominantly Anglo congregations."

The Rt. Rev. Todd Ousley of the Diocese of Eastern Michigan crafted this response: "Our diocese has fifty congregations with no priests of color serving in any congregations. Over the past five years, thirty-one calls have been issued for rectors or interim rectors with no persons of color being called. . . . In these searches, persons of color were intentionally identified to be included in each search." He went on to write that in three cases priests of color were among the finalists but withdrew, most likely due to two factors: diocesan demographics (in which few people of color reside) and a low diocesan salary scale.

The Rev. Gregory Jacobs writes: "We have been giving some thought to requiring anti-racism/diversity appreciation as part of the search process. I'm afraid we are not doing as good a job in this diocese as I would like, but we labor on. . . . We have 193 congregations. Here's what we have (in terms of rectors/vicars/priests-in-charge): Two men of color (Hispanics) serving culturally-mixed congregations (majority white), one as rector and one as priest-in-charge; one man (African American) serving as rector of a predominantly white congregation, one man (African American) serving as co-rector with his wife (who is white) in a predominantly white congregation."

The Rev. Mary Carson of the Diocese of Ohio writes: "We have one African priest who is rector of a three-parish shared ministry in rural northwestern Ohio. That represents approximately 2 to 3 percent of our 96 congregations."

The Rev. Canon Mary Sulerud tells us: "In the Diocese of Washington, four rectors who are persons of color have been called to predominately Caucasian congregations, the last in 2001. This represents 2.4 percent of our congregations."

The Rev. Canon Ernie Bennett of the Diocese of Central Florida responds: "None that I am aware of [clergy of color leading primarily Caucasian congregations]. We do have one black priest who is vicar of a very mixed congregation and one white priest serving an almost all black congregation."

The Rev. Canon Mark Dunnam of the Diocese of Central Gulf Coast writes: "We have in the diocese a Commission on Racial Reconciliation . . . but we do not require Search Committees to do anti-racism training. At present we have no person of color as rector of a predominately Caucasian congregation.... We do have a Caucasian priest at a predominately black congregation."

The Rev. Faith Perrizo of the Diocese of West Virginia responds: "Our one clergy of color is deployed in a cluster of six churches. Only one congregation is African American, the other five are Caucasian."

The Rev. Clarence Langdon responds: "In Chicago during the past two years we have had one African American priest called to a large predominately Caucasian congregation."

Colonel Forest S. Rittgers of the Diocese of Albany reported that out of 116 congregations, all of which are predominantly white, two are led by priests of color.

In the Diocese of West Tennessee, the Rev. Rene Somodevilla states that there is one African American serving as rector of a Caucasian parish.

Calls received across color lines are still rare. Might your congregation be called to change this reality? Women are still less likely to be called to lead vibrant, large churches. What about yours? Are you open to considering both male and female candidates equally? How about clergy over the age of sixty? Older clergy are being called to lead fewer congregations as newly ordained priests, even though many plan to work until the age of seventy-two. Could your congregation benefit from the wisdom and life experience of a cleric in this age group?

The one "ism" I have not yet discussed is one that I care about deeply. Homosexual and lesbian clergy are routinely discriminated against in our Discernment Process, with a number of congregations and some dioceses refusing to interview them for theological reasons. I have no statistics here because there are not any official statistics. I did not conduct my own survey, because there are still a number of dioceses in the Episcopal Church where the names of practicing homosexual and lesbian clergy are not allowed to be considered by the diocesan bishop. If this is approved in your diocese, wherever you find yourself on the theological spectrum, I pray that your committee will interview all viable candidates, regardless of their sexual orientation. While this is currently a divisive and painful issue in our church, it does not have to be so within your congregation. Please give this your prayerful and thoughtful consideration, treating each candidate who comes to you as the child of God she/he was created to be.

My prayer for each of you is best expressed in the poem "Prisms," written by Katharine Tyler Scott in 1984.

Isms
Fit best in prisms
Perceptions from different angles
Reflecting the light of truth
and brilliance of color
All different
and of Supreme value

Changes,
bringing different hues
from scattered penetration

The light from within and without
So pure
So true
So lovely
So DIFFERENT

To block the light
casts a shadow
To choose one lens
limits our vision
While not destroying truth,
will keep us from experiencing
the wholeness of what we and
others are

While not destroying differences
will create an illusion of sameness

while not destroying our spirits
will imprison them.

Divorced from diversity
Robbed of richness
Exempt from life's fullest experience
Shallow souls in search

The power to see yourself and
the "selves" of others
awaits you
deep inside.

You have the power to
Shape the view
Create the angle
Reflect the light
Transform isms to prisms.[3]

---

3. "Prisms," © 1984 by Katharine Tyler Scott. From the *Creative Journey Retreat* booklet (New York: Office of Women's Ministries, ECC, 1984), 76–77. Used with permission of the author.

Sample Meetings

◆ *First Discernment Committee Task Cluster*

From the following sample meetings, pick and choose what is needed for your Discernment Process as outlined by your diocesan Transition Ministries Officer. Before beginning, make sure you know your diocese's procedure for submitting names of candidates to your committee: What are the sources of the names? Will they be vetted prior to your receiving them? Will candidates contact your church directly or go through your diocesan office? At what point are you to let your diocese know the names of finalists for detailed background checking? Regular communication with your diocesan office will save your committee valuable time as your Discernment Process progresses.

In addition, make sure you are clear about your charge from the vestry: How many names of candidates do they want from your committee? Do they want them ranked by preference? Also, what is your budget now that the profile is complete?

I. Recapture the prayerful tone established on the Discerning Your Gifts Retreat. Begin with prayer and choose a Spiritual Guide as your first task. Who among you has been given special gifts of prayer and discernment? Whom do you trust to help you listen for the movements of the Spirit among you? Discuss as a group and reach a decision, praying for the guidance of the Holy Spirit.

Your Spiritual Guide can use one of the prayer methods discussed in Resource 1 at each meeting. For this gathering, pass around a special object like a rock, cross, prayer beads, symbol of your church, or any religious object. The person holding it prays silently for about five to ten minutes, while the meeting is in session. She/he then passes it to the next person, who begins praying silently. Continue until the meeting ends.

II. Work on team building.
   a. What are your expectations as our work begins? What are your hopes and fears?
   b. What spiritual gift was discerned in you at the retreat? How do you see yourself using it on this committee? *Or*
   Why did you say "yes" to this call? What might we look out for in working with you?

III. Develop group norms, such as: pray creatively throughout the meetings; pray daily for committee members and their work; begin and end all meetings on time; attend all meetings unless chairperson is called in advance; complete all assigned tasks on time; maintain confidentiality; communicate openly and honestly; listen with understanding; do not monopolize or force one's opinion.

IV. Discuss the following:
   a. *People who are here to serve as resources for you:*
      1. Your diocesan Transition Ministries Officer.
      2. Your Transition Consultant, if you have one. She/he can: 1) explain how she/he came to be with you and his/her role in the group; 2) explore your expectations of a Transition Consultant and clarify if necessary.
   b. *The vestry mandate.*
   c. *Your role as a Discernment Committee in an advisory capacity to the vestry.* Keep in mind that you will not be recommending someone for your vestry to hire. When a person is hired she/he works for you in an employee/employer relationship. This is not on any level the relationship between priest and congregation. Rather, you and your priest are here to manifest the body of Christ in your community together. You are here to serve each other and those around you. You are mutually accountable for the ministry you undertake together. Neither of you answers solely to the other.
   In a Discernment Process, which will be discussed in detail in the second task cluster, you need to look not only at the question of who has the skills needed to lead a congregation your size, but who is truly a person of prayer who can lead your church to a deeper knowledge of God. Whom could you trust? Who seems genuine to you and is willing to be vulnerable?
   d. *Your diocesan Affirmative Action policy.* Early in its existence, the Church Deployment Board of the Episcopal Church issued a statement of nondiscrimination against anyone on the basis of race, marital status, age, or sex. Check to see if your parish's computer profile has the box checked for "Applications from Women and Minorities Especially

Welcome." If so (and most churches do), you will receive a list of candidates that intentionally includes women and men, blacks, whites, Hispanics, Asians, and other people of color. Now is a good time to discuss being open to hiring a priest of a different gender or race than your former rector/vicar and to discuss the contents of the previous chapter, "'Isms' in the Discernment Process." Women, people of color, older clerics looking for a first call, and homosexual clergy are still routinely discriminated against in the Discernment Process. Discuss how your committee and vestry might begin to reverse this trend.

I am sometimes asked, "Should we decide ahead of time as a committee if we will hire an openly gay or lesbian priest?" I am clear in such circumstances that asking this question of a candidate is not only against the law, but making such a decision before meeting the candidates can lead the committee to become embroiled in a debate that can derail the process. I advise committees to meet with everyone who might be a fit without regard to race, gender, age, or sexual orientation; to treat each person as a child of God and see where the Holy Spirit is leading them.

I strongly recommend the ninety-minute Anti-Racism Workshop included here for your meeting prior to the telephone and face-to-face interviews. Alternatively, your diocese may have an Anti-Racism Committee that could conduct the training for you. However it is carried out, it is important that your Discernment Committee and vestry seriously discuss anti-racism as a group and learn more about it together. To move beyond the present statistics in our church requires intentionality on the part of each and every Discernment Committee.

e. *Issues of confidentiality.* Once your committee receives names of candidates, those candidates' vocations are literally in your hands. Many of them will be in churches who do not know they are in the Discernment Process for another call. For their current parish to learn "through the grapevine" that their priest is looking elsewhere can be devastating to all involved. This means that names are to be discussed ONLY with other Discernment Committee members, your Transition Ministries Officer, or your bishop. They are not to be discussed with your interim priest, your spouse or family members, your friend in another state. You would be surprised at how small the Episcopal Church really is.

f. *Sources of names of candidates* and the process by which you will receive them, after checking with your diocesan office.

g. *Method of background checking* used by your diocese, including the cost to your parish. This is critical, as results of the check usually must be received before your bishop can approve a call and the call can be announced to your parish. Nothing is more frustrating than having to

delay your announcement for several weeks or a month as you await
the results of the background check.

  h. *Common mistakes to avoid:*

- Removing names from the list of candidates at the CDO profile
  level.
- One or two Discernment Committee members dominating the
  Discernment Process.
- Overfocusing on one ideological or theological point.
- Stereotyping people you know.
- Being driven by anxiety.
- Overcompensating for perceived weaknesses in the former rector
  or vicar and calling that person's opposite.[4]

Committee members may want to make their own additions to this list.

V. Initial tasks to be completed:

  a. *Choose a primary contact person.* Often the member selected is chair
of the committee. Keep in mind that *this person might very well be the
most important person to the entire search process.* She or he needs to be
someone who loves to talk with people and connects easily and quickly with them. This is the person with whom the candidates will have the
most personal contact. It is essential that she/he is fully functional on
email. This person will be the primary contact person with all the candidates with both good and bad news.

  b. *Choose a correspondence secretary.* This member will be responsible
for all written communication to the candidates other than emails.

  c. *Choose a recording secretary* to take minutes at all meetings, with
confidential information omitted.

  d. *Choose a communication person* to maintain communication with
your Transition Ministries Officer, the vestry, and the congregation as
to where you are in the process. Keep the congregation apprised
through regular communication. (See "Mountain Climber Poster,"
Resource 7, or the committee might want to set up a Discernment
Committee bulletin board.)

VI. Debrief. A large amount of information has been shared and many
decisions made. Check in with members on how they feel after this
first gathering.

*Your Spiritual Guide closes the meeting by asking people how it felt to pray
throughout. How did you feel when praying? Did it change the meeting in any
way to know that someone was praying at all times?*

---

4. Overcompensating can result in calling a priest without a basic skill (taken for granted in the former
rector or vicar) that is both expected by parishioners and needed in the parish. This can result in a short
stay for the rector or vicar called, whereby she/he becomes an unintentional interim. List adapted from
material provided by the Rev. Richard J. Kirk, Organizational Consultant for Congregations.

◆ *Second Discernment Committee Task Cluster*

Your Spiritual Guide begins the meeting.

Now that the nuts and bolts of your Discernment Process are in place, it is important to spend a meeting focusing on the process of discernment. As recommended in the Introduction, many of you will have read Discerning God's Will Together: A Spiritual Practice for the Church *by Danny E. Morris and Charles M. Olsen. Their work provides the framework for this gathering.*

I. Morris and Olsen write: "God's will is obviously a higher value than the other values that motivate us: efficiency, expediency, unity at any cost, ego, politics, economics, charity, or concern about what other people think.... Even one person can weaken or derail spiritual discernment if he or she holds on to motivations other than the ultimate one of knowing God's will."[5] Discuss the following questions in groups of two:

   1. Has there been a time when you have been able to "discern the will of the Holy Spirit in your life"? What was that like for you? What did you have to give up?
   2. Has there been a time in the life of your parish when you have listened carefully for the will of God, then acted on that will? What was that like? If you cannot recall such an experience in the corporate life of your congregation, what might have gotten in the way of that?

II. We are all human, with human foibles and needs. None of us can escape our humanity! We might deny it, but we can't escape it. Discuss the following questions as a group:

   1. What might get in the way of your being able to totally turn your individual will over to God's will in the Discernment Process for a new rector or vicar?
   2. What might help?

III. Morris and Olsen point out that a solid spiritual base precedes the ability to discern the will of God.[6] Letting the Holy Spirit into your life, in whatever way you define that, is a necessary first step. Discuss the following questions in your original groups of two:

   1. Have you ever had an experience of the Holy Spirit? What was that like?

---

5. Danny E. Morris and Charles M. Olsen, *Discerning God's Will Together: A Spiritual Practice for the Church* (Bethesda, Md.: The Alban Institute, Inc., 1997), 39.
6. Morris and Olsen, *Discerning God's Will Together,* 41.

2. What is your current spiritual practice? Are you willing to talk with a member of the clergy about this as you go through this process?

IV. A key component of group discernment is what the Greeks called *metanoia,* meaning a change of heart. It may not happen that everyone on your committee discerns the same thing. If that occurs, how will you respond?

Morris and Olsen write: "Once we feel that we have received the gift of discernment, once we feel that we know God's will in a particular situation, are we willing to make the appropriate response? Or will we walk away?"[7] Questions to ponder in silence:

1. Has there ever been a time in your life when you discerned the will of God, but for some reason could not or did not act on it? What got in the way for you? How might this time be different?

2. Where do you stand personally regarding issues of gender, race, age, or sexual orientation in the Discernment Process? Are you open to all of God's children? Are you comfortable with where you are?

V. I can imagine that some of you at this point may be wondering what you've gotten yourself into. Good! Attempting to discern God's will is meant to stretch us, make us grow, challenge us. This process stretched the apostles who were often confused; it has stretched countless saints and mystics in the tradition of our church. You are meant to follow in their footsteps. Remember, there is a reason you were asked to serve on the Discernment Committee. Someone sees something in you that perhaps you do not yet see. Stick with it; pray; transformation does happen.

Your Spiritual Guide closes the meeting.

7. Morris and Olsen, *Discerning God's Will Together,* 41.

Discerning God's Will

There is nothing more challenging or rewarding than taking the time to try with all your heart to discern God's will in your life. Such discernment takes time, a great deal of patience, commitment to regular prayer and meditation, and often the input of another person. Why? Because there are many, many voices we hear in the midst of such discernment that are not the voice of God. One bishop remarked to the chair of his diocese's Commission on Ministry, "Why is it that the voice so many people hear and believe is God's voice sounds amazingly like their own?" And that is the question.

We are all influenced by the culture in which we live. Western individualism is not a meaningless textbook term, but a potent reality. We have been shaped by a culture that puts the individual at the center, rather than the common good. It is no wonder that when we enter into a time of discernment, either individual or corporate, we tend to lean toward that which is best for us personally. I know of no greater struggle as a Christian than this. Discerning God's will and leading in our life is not a one-time task. It is a lifelong process of continually asking if what we are doing is in accord with God's will. It is being willing to empty ourselves of our own preconceived notions, desires, and ego needs long enough to let God in. There is no room for God to act when we are filled to the brim with our own certainties of what God wants us to do or be.

As you enter more deeply into the period of discerning whom God is calling to lead your congregation at this particular time in your history, you might ask yourself the following questions:

1. Am I willing to let something die in me in order to give God room to start something new?

2. What will I need to lay aside or leave behind to be open to new gifts of God's grace or new expressions of ministry?[8]

These are tough questions, as tough as they get, because it is not in our nature to serve the common good by willingly letting go of something that is deeply important to us. It is in the nature of many of us to fight for what we believe in. We only have to look at current political

8. Adapted from Morris and Olsen, *Discerning God's Will Together,* 78–79.

history to see this reality lived out on a day-to-day basis. This political reality is often mirrored in the church and what I am suggesting is that you reverse that trend in the microcosm of your Discernment Committee. Not just stop it, but reverse it by living into a different way of being church together.

As you listen prayerfully to the other members of your Discernment Committee in the weeks and months ahead, you might want to keep asking yourself one question: *What is best for our church as a whole?* Not, what will advance the particular cause or area of the church for which I care most deeply, but what, and specifically *whom,* is God calling us to move forward in this process?

Honesty with yourself about where you are in the process of letting go is key. Honesty with members of your committee is equally important. If you're not there yet, if you're still holding on to a particular ideal or desire, be honest with your other committee members about that. It is nothing to be ashamed of. We all start out there and sometimes stay there! If you do not confide in others where you really stand, it will become obvious as the discussions unfold, so it's best to be upfront about it and go from there.

I am praying that each person who reads this book will at least give it his/her best try. One Discernment Committee said to me in all sincerity, "Look at us! We're a bunch of business people. We can't do this!" To which I replied with equal sincerity, "Yes, you can, with God's help." If you find yourself needing support with this, ask for it. There are many people—clergy and laity alike—who would be honored and delighted to help you.

Almighty God, to you all hearts are open, all desires known, and from you no secrets are hid: Help me not to hide from myself. Open my heart to your will for me and for my congregation. Help me to see where my own desires, needs, and motivations may be getting in the way. Empty me; purify me; guide me as I seek to serve your will and your will alone. As I pray the Lord's Prayer help me to hear anew the familiar words, "Your will be done on earth as it is in heaven." Amen.

Sample Meeting

◆ *Third Discernment Committee Task Cluster*

We're back to more nuts and bolts now, but keep the discernment issues of the last gathering always in your mind as the more task-oriented aspects of your Discernment Process continue.

This task cluster should occur after you have been given your final list of candidates. Once you have your final list and begin the process, it is best to close out your list. Each candidate deserves to be treated like every other candidate. Therefore, all should enter and go through the different stages of the process at the same time. Your ability to discern whom God is calling to lead your church will be greatly hampered if some candidates enter the process at a different time than others.

Your Spiritual Guide begins the meeting.

I. Discuss with your Transition Consultant or diocesan Transition Ministries Officer the steps of your Discernment Process from this point forward. Each diocese will have a different process, but many will include the following elements:
- Emailing and mailing information about your congregation to each candidate, with no more than three short questions for the candidate to answer.
- Carefully reviewing candidates' responses, then group discernment of whom to move forward.
- Telephone conversations with candidates, depending on proximity (group discernment).
- Face-to-face meetings (group discernment).
- Site visits to three to five candidates, depending on budget.
- Group discernment of final two to three candidates.

- Candidates make parish visits with Discernment Committee (group discernment).
- Candidates make parish visits with vestry and bishop (vestry discernment).
- Establish a timeline with dates for each step of the process, and share it with your vestry and candidates.

II. Set up confidential files for each member of the Discernment Committee. Each member can have one folder for each candidate containing all information received on that individual. (One person can be in charge of copying all information received for each person.) In addition, there can be a master file kept by the chair of the Discernment Committee. Individual committee members can keep all their notes and reflections on each candidate in their file.[9]

Never leave these files at the church. I once found a Discernment Committee member's file folders accidentally left on a table in the narthex where anyone in the parish could have picked them up. It cannot be stressed enough that the integrity of your entire Discernment Process will depend on strict methods of confidentiality.

On the other hand, don't go too far in the other direction. One Discernment Committee was so concerned about confidentiality that only the chair of the committee was allowed to have files. Individual members had to go to his home and check out the file folders, then return them. As a result, the Discernment Process took twice as long as it might have and they lost several good candidates to other churches.

III. Review initial paperwork received on the candidates.
  a. Discuss how to read and interpret clergy Church Deployment Office (CDO) profiles with either your Transition Consultant or diocesan contact, and then review them. Keep in mind that *no candidate should be removed from your process solely on the basis of the CDO profile. It was never intended for that use.* It is a self-reporting device that can only impart very general information. Look most closely at the personal statement on the profile and any other personal information you have received.

One parish devised an elaborate grid that they matched to each person's profile, and then removed those names that did not fit in the grid. Please do not do this! Many good, viable candidates were removed from this parish's list for the wrong reasons. This was never the intention of the CDO profile; it should not be misused in this way.

As of this writing, the Church Deployment Office at the Episcopal Church Center is working on a different type of clergy profile that will replace the current CDO profile. When that occurs, your diocesan office or Transition Consultant will be able to familiarize you with it.

9. Richard L. Ullman, *Choosing to Serve: Resources for the Calling Process* (New York: The Church Deployment Board of the Episcopal Church, 1991), V-7.

IV. Have your contact person establish email contact with all candidates as soon as possible. This immediately sets a caring, responsive tone. Let them know you have received their material and when they will next hear from you. Next, send the cover letter with questions via email, letting them know that a hard copy with additional information will be sent via snail mail.

V. Your initial mailing to each candidate might include the following:
a. *Cover letter with questions for candidates* (see sample in Resource 12). Make sure the cover letter has a deadline for getting the answers back that allows a reasonable amount of time for the candidate to respond, keeping in mind major seasonal celebrations in the church year. There should be no more than three questions with a maximum seventy-five-word response for each. While it is best to write your own questions, here are some suggestions to get you started:
1. Describe the most rewarding ministry project you have led in the last five years.
2. Describe your leadership style and give an example.
3. Tell us what you like best and least about your current position.
b. *Your church's CDO profile, and written profile or website information.*[10]
c. *Materials describing your congregation:* parish brochure, church bulletins, annual reports, newsletters, special events programs.
d. *"Chamber of Commerce" materials.*
e. *Video, if desired.* John Vonhof states: "A well-made videotape will show more to your candidates about your church and congregational life than any other medium. Activities and subjects to videotape include: choir practices, children and youth programs, fellowship groups, vacation Bible school, church school or Sunday school, special choir cantatas; casual interviews with church members; and the church grounds, facilities, and rectory/vicarage. Include an introduction of board [vestry] members and a time for search committee members to be introduced and share their thoughts. Be sure the search committee views the videotape so they know what the candidates will see. Keep it less than an hour in length."[11]
f. *Self-addressed, stamped postcard* for candidates to indicate their intention regarding your Discernment Process. Make sure that this and all correspondence from candidates is not addressed to your church, but to either a personal or business address of one of the Discernment Committee members. This is very important in terms of confidentiality. The return address of any material mailed back to the church can be

10. Timothy K. Vance, "Some Advice for Search Committees," *The Living Church* (September 2000), 25. Vance writes, "Any first contact should include the congregation's CDO profile. This simple document contains a wealth of information that most clergy know how to read. It allows one to size up a congregation, comparing apples to apples and oranges to oranges."
11. John Vonhof, *Pastoral Search: The Alban Guide to Managing the Pastoral Search Process* (Washington, D.C.: The Alban Institute, 1999), 33.

read by anyone sorting the mail. Also, a personal or business fax number and email address should be included, not your church's.

VI. Once candidates respond favorably, frequent and thorough communication with them is highly important. *It is important to communicate with the candidates at least once every two weeks. Communication can make or break a Discernment Process.* Throughout the process clergy will be taking stock of how well your committee communicates with them and how they are treated in general. Most clergy know that the way they are treated during a Discernment Process is the way they are likely to be treated should they accept a call to your parish.

Your Spiritual Guide closes the meeting.

Anti-Racism Workshop

This workshop is intended as an introduction to anti-racism training for Discernment Committees, vestries, and congregations and is meant to serve as a catalyst for further education and/or action. In addition, I recommend that parishioners read *Life on the Color Line* by Gregory Howard Williams, the true story of a white boy who discovered he was black.[12] Williams's book is one the most compelling and thought-provoking I have read. Each page brims with insight into the struggle of African Americans in our country.

The two-hour Anti-Racism Workshop included here has been prepared with the busy lay leader or cleric in mind. All the information needed to present the workshop is provided; detailed instructions allow facilitators with limited preparation time or teaching experience to use this program with confidence.

The workshop can be used with an adult or teen group of up to eighty to one hundred people or with a group as small as six. As with any educational tool, make it your own by adapting it to your teaching style and to the unique needs of your committee or congregation. A variety of teaching styles have been incorporated—experiential, lecture, small group discussion, writing—in order to reach as many people as possible.

The use of team facilitators is recommended, as two people will bring differing skills and perspectives. It is particularly important in a workshop on anti-racism to have a person of color and a white person working together. It is also preferable to have one woman and one man. Your priest, Transition Consultant, Anti-Racism Coordinator for your diocese, or other trained individuals can be consulted about possibly facilitating this workshop for your committee. It should be led by someone who is not a member of your vestry or Discernment Committee.

The purpose of this workshop is to help open dialogue between participants from differing ethnic backgrounds. It is, therefore, very

---

12. Gregory Howard Williams, *Life on the Color Line* (New York: The Penguin Group, 1995). Of this book the *New York Times Book Review* writes, "A stunning perspective on racial oppression and identity, [Williams's] recollections are precise, balanced, and well written." The *Buffalo News* writes, "Captivating…not since the classic *Black Like Me* have the issues of race and identity been explored from a place so close to the heart."

important to have a group that represents a diversity of people. Your vestry and Discernment Committee will, I hope, be made up of people from different ethnic backgrounds. If this is difficult within your congregation, please consider inviting members of another congregation to join you—from either an Episcopal church or another denomination in your vicinity.

Here are a few practical suggestions that may help you implement the program. Your facilitators should greet people warmly when they arrive and be available for informal questions and concerns before and after the session. Racism is not an easy subject for most people to discuss. Since your group will be small, you can seat people in a circle. This encourages mutual sharing and helps integrate the facilitators into the group.

MATERIALS NEEDED — Construction paper cut into fourths, enough for one piece per participant
Paper and pen for each person
Nametags for everyone
Whiteboard and marker
Drinks and light snacks

AGENDA

I. Introduction: To Respect the Dignity of Every Human Being[13] *(15 minutes)*

II. Being on the Outside: A Meditation *(15 minutes)*

III. Free Association: Definitions of Racism *(5 minutes)*

IV. The Global Hierarchy of Race *(25 minutes)*

Break (10 minutes)

V. A Personal Inventory: Recruitment into Racism *(25 minutes)*

VI. The Legacy of White Privilege *(20 minutes)*

VI. Wrap-Up *(5 minutes)*

I. INTRODUCTION:
TO RESPECT THE DIGNITY OF EVERY HUMAN BEING
As your Discernment Committee begins the process of meeting with prospective candidates for rector or vicar of your church, it is important to deal openly and honestly with the issue of institutional racism that exists throughout institutional structures in America, including

---

13. If desired, the Introduction can be given as a handout, with the oral presentation highlighting key points of the address.

the church. A very small percentage of clergy of color are called to lead predominately Caucasian congregations. Yet in some of our dioceses, Caucasians are actually in the minority. Anti-racism training is required of every Discernment Committee in the Diocese of New Jersey. This requirement, along with trained anti-racism leaders giving workshops throughout the diocese, has resulted in the calling of six priests of color to lead predominately Caucasian congregations in the last two years: four African Americans (which include both Africans and Caribbeans), one Hispanic, and one Indian (subcontinent).

While few churchgoers today would classify themselves as racist, it is systemic racism that is the issue. In his book *Outrage and Hope,* the Rt. Rev. Frederick Borsch, retired bishop of the Diocese of Los Angeles, writes, "Few people want to believe that they have racist attitudes and engage in racist actions, but few are the people who escape them. Indeed the most dangerous racists in our society may be those who think they are not."[14]

In order to help us all look honestly at ourselves and our church in terms of racism, education is needed, as learning and re-learning attitudes and assumptions is a lifelong process. To aid you in this journey at this critical time of transition in our congregation, this workshop is being offered.

It is helpful to begin with one basic question: "How does the Christian tradition inform our response to this issue?" As Episcopalians, we have a three-legged stool of authority—scripture, tradition, and reason. What insights from these areas of authority might inform our understanding of the issue of racism?

What the Prayer Book Says
"Will you strive for justice and peace among all people, and respect the dignity of every human being?" (BCP 305). This question from the Baptismal Covenant states succinctly and poignantly what it means to be a Christian. Not only respect for the dignity of all human beings, but justice for all as well lies at the heart of the Christian faith and is central to the theology of the 1979 *Book of Common Prayer.* As Episcopalians, we renew our baptismal vows each time we witness a baptism, reminding us that justice for all was not only central to Jesus' ministry but must be central to ours as well.

This theology has its roots in creation, as articulated in the 1979 Prayer Book. The Catechism states: "All people are worthy of respect and honor, because all are created in the image of God" (BCP 846). The creation of all humanity in God's image is emphasized in our Eucharistic Prayers as well: Eucharistic Prayer II, Rite I states: "All glory be to thee, O Lord our God, for that thou didst create heaven and earth,

---

14. Frederick Houk Borsch, *Outrage and Hope: A Bishop's Reflections in Times of Change and Challenge* (Valley Forge, Pa.: Trinity Press International, 1996), 16.

and didst make us in thine own image" (BCP 341); Eucharistic Prayer D, Rite II states: "Your mighty works reveal your wisdom and love. You formed us in your own image" (BCP 373). This belief is stated further in a number of prayers: "For the Mission of the Church" (BCP 206, 257); "For Social Justice" (BCP 209, 260); the first Preface of the Lord's Day (BCP 344, 377); and in the opening prayer of the service for the Dedication and Consecration of a Church (BCP 567). Clearly, the understanding that all people everywhere are created in God's image and are therefore worthy of equal respect and honor is a theme that runs throughout the 1979 *Book of Common Prayer.*

This theology is affirmed in the Prayer Book not only in reference to God as creator but to God as the incarnate Christ. The Preface of the Incarnation states, "O God, who wonderfully created, and yet more wonderfully restored, the dignity of human nature: Grant that we may share the divine life of him who humbled himself to share our humanity, your Son Jesus Christ" (BCP 252). Thus, the dignity of human nature, defiled by sin following creation, has been restored through the incarnation of Jesus Christ. For us to deny that dignity in any way is to deny the efficacy of the incarnation itself.

In addition, justice for all, regardless of race, gender, age, nationality, or sexual orientation, is held up to God in the prayer "For the Oppressed," which begins, "Look with pity, O heavenly Father, upon the people in this land who live with injustice, terror, disease, and death as their constant companions." It continues, "Strengthen those who spend their lives establishing equal protection of the law and equal opportunities for all" (BCP 826).

Furthermore, the Catechism states clearly that "the mission of the Church is to restore all people to unity with God and each other in Christ" (BCP 855). Thus, confronting and disassembling racism is central to our mission as a church. Christ came to restore the original intention of God in creation; as the body of Christ, we are to embody that new creation.

What Scripture Says
The creation of all people in the image of God is a significant component of Prayer Book theology, which has its roots in Holy Scripture. The first creation account in Genesis states, "So God created humankind in his image, in the image of God he created them; male and female he created them.... God saw everything that he had made, and indeed, it was very good" (Gen. 1:27, 31). Thus, there are no distinctions among people in the original creation. It is only after Adam and Eve exercise their free will and try to be as knowledgeable as God that a statement of inequality occurs, and it is between male and

female. It is important to note that there are no distinctions in the created order. Then, as now, God is working in history to try to re-create each one of us and to restore right relationships among us, relationships that are reflective of the original intent of creation.

To restore humanity to the purpose for which it was created, God came to earth as the incarnate Christ. Thus, it is important to look closely at the life and teachings of Jesus of Nazareth.

When Jesus read from the scroll of the prophet Isaiah in the synagogue in Nazareth, he made it clear that his ministry was for everyone, especially the oppressed. "The Spirit of the Lord is upon me, because he has anointed me to bring good news to the poor. He has sent me to proclaim release to the captives and recovery of sight to the blind, to let the oppressed go free, to proclaim the year of the Lord's favor" (Luke 4:18–19).

In addition, a guiding principle in determining the authority of a given portion of scripture is the statement of Jesus in Matthew known as the Rule of Love. "'You shall love the Lord your God with all your heart, and with all your soul, and with all your mind.' This is the greatest and first commandment. And a second is like it: 'You shall love your neighbor as yourself.' On these two commandments hang all the law and the prophets" (Matt. 22:37–40). This saying of Jesus is repeated at the beginning of the Holy Eucharist, Rite I (BCP 324) and the Penitential Order, Rite I (BCP 319).

Furthermore, the writings of St. Paul clearly and succinctly state our responsibilities as Christian people. In his letter to the Galatians, he writes, "In Christ Jesus you are all children of God through faith. As many of you as were baptized into Christ have clothed yourselves with Christ. There is no longer Jew or Greek, there is no longer slave or free, there is no longer male and female; for all of you are one in Christ Jesus" (Gal. 3:26–28). Just as there are to be no distinctions among people in the original creation, there are to be no distinctions in the new creation.

How are we, as Christians, to live into this reality? St. Paul tells us, "For just as the body is one and has many members, and all the members of the body, though many, are one body, so it is with Christ. For in the one Spirit we were all baptized into one body—Jews or Greeks, slaves or free—and we were all made to drink of one Spirit." He goes on to write, "If one member suffers, all suffer together with it; if one member is honored, all rejoice together with it" (1 Cor. 12:12–13, 26). We become part of the body of Christ through baptism. When part of the body of Christ is denied justice because of race, or any other issue, all parts of the body suffer; all are hurt. We are not to respond to injustice as though we are separate one from another, for we are all one as members of the body of Christ.

God has spoken clearly through the words of scripture as to God's intention for all of humanity. God has spoken through the actions of Jesus, time and again, against structures that limit the freedom of people to be who they were created by God to be, in God's image, as recorded in scripture and articulated throughout the 1979 *Book of Common Prayer.*

What Anglican Tradition Says
The most definitive positions on justice within the Anglican Communion can be found by looking at resolutions passed by the Lambeth Conference, which has met once each decade since 1867. This conference has passed a number of resolutions in favor of basic human rights. The Encyclical Letter of the 1908 conference teaches of "the inestimable value of every human being in the sight of God, and His special thought for the weak and the oppressed."[15] Similarly, the 1948 Lambeth Conference stated: "The Christian doctrine of man is the true justification of the recognition of human rights. According to this doctrine every individual man is of supreme value in the sight of God, for he is made in the image of God, he is called to be a child of God, for his sake Christ died, and his heritage is life eternal. Every man must have freedom to respond to the call of God and be given opportunities whereby the whole of his personality may be fully developed to the glory of God. Without these elementary rights man cannot use completely the talents with which God has endowed him."[16]

Again in 1978, the Lambeth Conference passed a resolution on human rights. Resolution 3 stated, "The conference regards the matter of human rights and dignity as of capital and universal importance.... We deplore and condemn the evils of racism and tribalism, economic exploitation and social injustice, torture, detention without trial and the taking of human lives as contrary to the teaching and example of our Lord in the Gospel."[17]

What are caring Christians to do when the church itself reflects institutional racism and does not reflect these basic tenets of our faith? It is helpful to look within the Anglican tradition itself for guidance. The Encyclical Letter of the Lambeth Conference of 1908 states: "Underlying it [the church] are ideals of brotherhood, liberty, and mutual justice and help. In those ideals we recognize the working of our Lord's teaching as to the inestimable value of every human being in the sight of God, and His special thought for the weak and the

---

15. G. R. Evans and J. Robert Wright, eds., *The Anglican Tradition* (Philadelphia: Fortress Press, 1991), 369.
16. Resolutions of the Lambeth Conference 1948, Part II, *Lambeth Conferences, 1867–1948* (London: SPCK, 1948), 13. Written in non-inclusive language in 1948.
17. Evans and Wright, eds., *Anglican Tradition,* 513–514.

oppressed. . . . We call upon the Church to consider how far and where-in it has departed from these truths."[18] *(You may want to write this quotation on whiteboard.)*

What Reason Might Say

Prayer Book theology is consistent regarding justice and equality for all, as is Anglican theology and Holy Scripture. This theology can only stand in opposition to institutional racism. People of faith must respond. If the theology of our worship is not lived out in practice within the church itself, something is indeed amiss.

Before any of us can adequately respond to this issue, we must look at ourselves, our attitudes and assumptions, for we are all, each and every one of us, part of the problem, just as we are all part of the solution. The rest of our program will focus on looking at ourselves, for we are where it all begins. We are where it all can end.

II. BEING ON THE OUTSIDE: A MEDITATION[19]

Note to facilitators: Before beginning this exercise, give each participant a piece of colored construction paper. Then give the following introduction:

As we all know, certain experiences can make people feel excluded. In our first exercise, we will walk through a meditation of our own experiences of being on the outside. What we would like you to do is take a few moments to remember when you were on the outside of something, really on the outside, and painfully aware of whatever it was that kept you there. *(Long pause.)*

Please take your piece of paper and write down a few words that remind you of the experience. No one will read these but you. *(Pause.)*

Now we'll take a few minutes to think about our experiences, so get comfortable and close your eyes, if you would like, as I lead us on a meditation of our own experiences of being on the outside. *(Pause.)*

Think of the feelings you associate with your experience. *(Pause.)*

Think about what those people on the inside looked like to you. *(Pause.)*

Think about what you looked like to those on the inside. *(Pause.)*

What were your thoughts about yourself at the time? *(Pause.)*

Finally, please take time to remember this experience. *(Pause.)*

To conclude our meditation, we would like to gather our feelings and experiences of being on the outside and put them in a basket. We will pass the basket around to each one of you. Please place your story of exclusion in the basket. When they are all gathered together, we will put them in the center of the group to symbolize their place among us.

---

18. Evans and Wright, eds., *Anglican Tradition*, 369.
19. Adapted from Elizabeth Rankin Geitz, Margaret Prescott, and Kerry Holder, *Recovering Lost Tradition* (Princeton: Trinity Church, 1988), 6.

The basket will stay visible throughout this session to symbolize our common bond as people who know what it means to be on the outside. We will then offer them up to God at our next Holy Eucharist as a church family.

III. FREE ASSOCIATION: DEFINITIONS OF RACISM[20]

On whiteboard, draw a large circle with lines radiating from it. In the middle of the circle write the word "Racism." Ask participants to free-associate with the word "racism." Write their responses at the end of each line.

IV. THE GLOBAL HIERARCHY OF RACE

Download "The Global Hierarchy of Race" by Martin Jacques from www.provinceviii.org by clicking on "icmd" and then on "anti-racism." Invite participants to read it aloud, with a different person reading each paragraph. Then discuss in pairs the following questions:

1. How did you feel listening to or reading this essay?
2. Have you ever experienced what Martin Jacques experienced, either himself or through the treatment of his wife?
3. If so, what was that like for you?

Encourage people to share with the larger group as they are comfortable. Then as a large group, discuss the following definition of racism:

Racism is Prejudice plus Power.[21]

1. In light of Jacques's article, would you agree or disagree? Why or why not?

V. A PERSONAL INVENTORY: RECRUITMENT INTO RACISM

If your group is large, divide participants into groups of eight to ten. Distribute Handout A. Give all participants a piece of paper and a pen; encourage them to write their own individual responses to the questions before sharing them with their group.

---

20. Adapted from Alice Sargeant, *Beyond Sex Roles* (Minnesota: West Publishing Co., 1977). All rights reserved. Quoted in Judith H. Katz, *White Awareness: Handbook for Anti-Racism Training* (Norman and London: University of Oklahoma Press, 1978), 48.

21. See Joseph A. Barndt, *Dismantling Racism: The Continuing Challenge to White America* (Minneapolis: Augsburg Fortress, 1991), chapter 2. Of Barndt's book, Joan B. Campbell, former General Secretary of the National Council of Churches, writes: "This book . . . helps us understand how our racism functions in, and is perpetrated in, our homes, schools, churches and institutions. It is a tough and demanding book that moves us through guilt and blame to effective action."

VI. THE LEGACY OF WHITE PRIVILEGE[22]

If your room is large enough, ask people to form a straight line down the middle at an equal distance from the walls. As you read each statement from Handout B, ask people to take a step to the right, if this description applies to them. If it does not, then they take a step to the left. (You may want to choose only ten statements to read if time is a factor. The effect is the same.) The advantage of having people move physically is to engage the whole body in the experience of privilege, rather than just the mind. When the statements have all been read, ask the following questions:

1. What strikes you first about this exercise?
2. What can you do with the privilege you have?

Give each person a copy of Handout B to share with their family or friends.

VII. WRAP-UP

Give participants an opportunity to share their feelings, any insights gained, and possible next steps.

---

22. Adapted from Jerry Drino, *Reclaiming the Beloved Community: Dialogue Across Scripture on Diversity, Ethnicity, and Justice* (Province VIII of the Episcopal Church: InterCultural Ministry Development, 1997). Used by permission of the author.

Handout A
A PERSONAL INVENTORY[23]

Please write your responses to the following questions on the paper provided before sharing with your group.

1. When were you first aware of racial and ethnic differences? What are your earliest recollections of how people of color were/are treated?

2. What kinds of contact did you have with people of different racial or ethnic backgrounds at the time you became aware of these differences?

3. How did important adults help you interpret your experiences?

4. How did you first experience racism? From where did you learn to identify it? What did it mean to you? How did it function in your perception of yourself? How did it make you feel? How did it affect you in relationship to other people?

5. How were you recruited into racism?

23. Adapted from Drino, *Reclaiming the Beloved Community.* Used by permission of the author. This handout may be downloaded from www.churchpublishing.org/callingclergy.

Handout B
UNDERSTANDING WHITE PRIVILEGE[24]

1. I can arrange to be in the company of people of my own ethnic group most of the time.
2. I can avoid spending time with people whom I was trained to mistrust and who have learned to mistrust my kind or me.
3. If I should need to move, I can be pretty sure of renting or purchasing a dwelling in an area that I can afford and in which I would want to live.
4. I can be pretty sure that my neighbors in such a location will be neutral or pleasant to me.
5. I can go shopping alone most of the time, pretty well assured that I will not be followed or harassed.
6. I can turn on the television or read the front page of the newspaper and see people of my ethnic group widely represented.
7. When I am told about our national heritage or about "civilization," I am shown that people of my color made it what it is.
8. If a traffic cop pulls me over or if the IRS audits my tax return, I can be sure I haven't been singled out because of my skin color.
9. I can arrange to protect my children most of the time from people who might not like them.
10. I can be pretty sure of having my voice heard in a group in which I am the only member of my ethnic group.
11. Whether I use checks, credit card, or cash, I can count on my skin color not to work against the appearance of financial responsibility.
12. I do not have to educate my children to be aware of systemic racism for their own protection.
13. I can be pretty sure my children will be well liked by their teachers, if they are obedient children. My chief worries about them do not concern societal attitudes about their ethnic group.
14. I can swear, or dress in secondhand clothes, or not answer letters, without having people attribute these choices to the bad morals, poverty, or illiteracy of my ethnic group.
15. I am never asked to speak for all the people of my ethnic group.
16. I can be pretty sure that if I ask to talk to the "person in charge" I will be facing a person of my own ethnic group.
17. I can choose blemish cover or bandages in "flesh" color and have them more or less match my skin color.

24. Adapted from Drino, *Reclaiming the Beloved Community.* Used by permission of the author. This handout may be downloaded from www.churchpublishing.org/callingclergy.

More Sample Meetings

◆ *Fourth Discernment Committee Task Cluster*

Your Spiritual Guide begins the meeting by sharing the type of prayer that will be used throughout.

As you develop questions and topics for your discussions with candidates, keep in mind the strengths of your congregation. It is best and more productive to build on strengths than to try to solve problems. This does not mean that problems do not need to be addressed, but your reality will become what you focus on. Focus on your strengths, not your weaknesses.

I. Begin by sharing with one another the single most exciting, energizing event or ministry that has occurred in your parish in the last two years. What makes this particular experience stand out from the others for you? How can you build on this foundation?

II. Develop topics for telephone conversations and face-to-face meetings:
    a. Using SPACEPOW (Resource 11) or the Nine Typical Areas in the Church Deployment Board booklet *Interviewing in the Calling Process*[25] (pages 13–20), prioritize the four most important areas of ministry in your congregation. Check these against the four areas listed on your parish position profile. If they are not the same, why not?
    b. Develop questions by using the following method:
        1. Break into small groups.
        2. Assign each small group one of the chosen areas from the SPACEPOW exercise. *Or*
        Use the Nine Typical Areas from *Interviewing in the Calling Process* to aid in writing questions.
        3. Review "Framing Questions" (pages 11–12) in *Interviewing in the Calling Process*.

---

25. The booklet may be ordered or downloaded from www.episcopalchurch.org/cdo.

4. Charge each small group to write two or three questions for telephone conversations that relate to their topic area and two or three questions for the face-to-face meetings. This should take no more than twenty-five minutes.

5. Re-form into a large group. Write each question on newsprint below an appropriate heading with two separate listings, one for the telephone questions and one for the face-to-face questions.

6. Post newsprint so it is visible.

7. Have the group go through each question for comments and revision so the group is satisfied with it.

8. Look for questions that could logically be combined.

9. Have the group decide on two or three questions for the telephone conversations and two or three questions for the face-to-face meetings. Committee members can put checkmarks by their three favorite questions in each category. Telephone conversations should last forty-five minutes to one hour. The initial face-to-face meeting should be no longer than sixty to ninety minutes and does not include the candidate's spouse or partner.

10. Once the two lists of questions are finalized, have the group prioritize them by once again putting a checkmark by their favorites. Each person has three checkmarks for each set of questions. This will provide the order the questions will be asked.

11. Once the questions are finalized, discuss specifically what you would like to tell the candidate about your congregation. What are your hopes and dreams? Your strengths? Areas where you need some help?

12. Share these questions and this information with the vestry.

III. Review information returned by the candidates and decide who might be called to lead your congregation. Are issues of age, gender, race, or sexual orientation a factor in your decision? Be aware of this possibility. Those candidates agreed on by the committee should be engaged in a telephone conversation at a mutually agreeable time. Send a letter to the candidate before the call is made with the names of Discernment Committee members. It is also helpful to state which person is going to ask which general area question (such as Christian education, preaching, and so on) and that you will also be sharing information with them that is important to you about your church.

I have never met a priest who likes telephone interviews. They are impersonal, and without being able to have eye contact, much is lost. It will be helpful, and your priest candidates will appreciate it, if you are willing to give them the questions ahead of time. This increases their comfort level and will communicate your care for them at this early stage in the process. There will be plenty of time later to ask the candidates questions that they will answer without advance preparation.

   Plan to give at least one-third of the allotted conversation time to the candidates to ask questions of your committee and to share anything about themselves they deem to be important. Remember, they are also in a Discernment Process. This type of give-and-take is central to mutual discernment.

Your Spiritual Guide closes the meeting.

◆ *Fifth Discernment Committee Task Cluster*

Your Spiritual Guide begins this gathering. You might want to rotate prayer throughout the group during each telephone conversation by passing a religious object from one person to another.

I. Telephone conversation

   a. This conversation is a cost-effective way of getting to know your candidates. It is not the time for a lot of personal questions, but rather for meaningful conversation designed around specific topic areas. The entire conversation should last no more than fifty to sixty minutes. It is possible to schedule up to four telephone conversations on a Saturday, with time in between to write impressions and take a break.

   b. Your Transition Consultant, if you have one, will not attend this or any other candidate meetings. The entire Discernment Committee does attend. Having each person on a true conference call (with his or her own telephone) is optimum, if money permits. Someone on the committee should serve as timekeeper.

   c. First, share the information about your church that you have agreed upon at the beginning of the conversation. Then each person in turn has five minutes to ask questions and get responses from the candidate. In other words, five minutes for Christian formation, five for stewardship, five for preaching, and so on. State at the

> "A search process is the first contact your new priest will have with your congregation. By attending to the details of this encounter, and by exhibiting Christian hospitality, a solid groundwork is laid for a long and fruitful relationship between priest and people." —Timothy K. Vance, "Some Advice for Search Committees," The Living Church (September 2000).

beginning of the conversation that the candidate will have twenty minutes at the end to ask his or her own questions of any committee members and discuss his or her ministry.

d. At the end of the conversation, be gracious. Let the candidates know how very much you appreciate their time in answering both your written questions and oral ones. *Then let the candidates know the timeline for the rest of your Discernment Process.*

e. Remember from this point on to maintain regular contact with each candidate still in your process. Contact should be made no less than every two weeks. This could mean the difference between a call that is accepted and one that is not. Some discernment committees assign a member to each candidate to be his or her contact person. In other cases, the chairperson or one contact person fulfills this role.

Praying with Intentionality

Having participated in a number of Discernment Committee meetings now, it is time to reflect on your feelings about this lay ministry in which you are so deeply involved. Do you find your interior life being affected by the process in any way? If so, how? If you are open to it, serving on a Discernment Committee can be a time of spiritual growth. On the other hand, if there is conflict among committee members, it can be a time of disillusionment. Monitor yourself as the process unfolds, being honest about how you really feel.

Is the Discernment Process taking more time than you thought? Is there openness among committee members or is something left unsaid that needs to be brought out into the open? If so, might you be the one to do so? It is my prayer that you will use this time of discernment on behalf of your congregation to grow in your own relationship with God. Consistent prayer and reflection throughout and being attentive to your personal needs will aid in this process.

As you reflect on your most recent discussion with the candidates, reimagine your conversation with each, to the extent that you can. Did you sense the presence of the Holy Spirit in some conversations and not others? What might have contributed to this difference? Is there one moment in a particular conversation that jumped out at you as authentic, resonating at some place deep within your soul? You might want to write it down. If that happened for you with some candidates and not others, focus on those in which it did occur. You might ask Jesus to join you in this time of reflection. How might he view each priest with whom you spoke or met?

Reflect on your Anti-Racism Workshop in light of conversations with candidates. Is there any learning from that workshop that helps you see a particular candidate in a new light? If so, share your insight with other committee members.

Next, picture your church filled with parishioners—all parishioners, those with whom you agree and those with whom you do not. What might they have heard if they had been privileged to be in on the conversation? Would significant groups in your church feel as you did?

Would they feel differently? How might this inform your Discernment Process?

Now picture those who are not yet members of your church—the people in your community without a church home. How might they feel about the candidates with whom you spoke? Which candidates might meet their needs?

Hold each candidate who spoke with you in prayer. Hold their families, loved ones, and current parishioners in prayer. Ask that God be with them as they, like you, discern where God is leading them. Reflect on each priest as a beloved child of God who has gifts to share. Which priest might best lead your parish in the areas of hospitality, healing, justice ministry? Which one do you discern is best able to lead your parishioners into a deeper union with God? Studies have shown that a focus on these areas of ministry leads to thriving, vital congregations. Intentional discernment in these areas will serve your parish well in the long run. Diana Butler Bass studied fifty thriving Episcopal congregations and discovered that a focus on these ministries led to vital, growing churches. Two other commonalities were a focus on tradition as fluid (retraditioning) and a focus on an energizing goal.[26] It is helpful to keep these in mind as you discern which candidate can best lead your parish into a vital, engaging tomorrow.

Now reflect on the strengths of your congregation as identified in the profile and in your Discernment Committee discussions. Which candidate seems to have the gifts to build on these strengths? Which seems to be the type of leader who could guide your church into the unknown territory of tomorrow? The rector or vicar of a parish needs to be someone who is not afraid to lead and who has the gifts to do so effectively.

At each step in the Discernment Process, the answers to these questions will become clearer. *I suggest reflecting on them after each set of interviews.* At each stage, be open to the movement of the Spirit in your life, in the communal life of the committee, and in the lives of the candidates. Expect to be surprised!

O God, who has made us creatures of time, so that every tomorrow is unknown country, and every decision a venture in faith: Grant us, frail children of the day, who are yet blind to the future, to move toward it in the sure confidence of your love, from which neither life nor death can ever separate us. Amen.

—Reinhold Niebuhr

26. See Bass, *The Practicing Congregation: Imagining a New Old Church.*

More Sample Meetings

◆ *Sixth Discernment Committee Task Cluster*

Your Spiritual Guide begins the meeting.

I. Preparation for face-to-face meetings
    a. Thoroughly discuss the material in *Interviewing in the Calling Process.* Keep in mind that the face-to-face meeting is for the purpose of *mutual* discernment and you should let the candidate know at the outset that your committee views it as such. In addition, your process "must allow opportunity for clergy to test whether they are truly called to this congregation as well as whether the parish feels they are the right priest. The phrase 'right priest' is important. Not just any 'good priest' will be the right 'fit' for your church."[27]

    Keep in mind that this meeting will leave either a positive or a negative impression with the candidate. For that reason, it is important to prepare and practice before you meet with any candidates.

    b. This meeting for a process of mutual discernment is quite different from interviewing someone in a secular work setting. Review page 3 in the Introduction for additional information.

    c. Practice asking questions, listening, answering possible candidate questions, and sharing information about your congregation. This can take up to two hours.

Your Spiritual Guide closes the meeting.

---

27. The Rev. Richard J. Kirk, Organizational Consultant for Congregations.

♦ *Seventh Discernment Committee Task Cluster*

Your Spiritual Guide begins the meeting.

I. Review the candidates' materials that have been returned, along with notes from the telephone conversations. Decide which candidates to move forward, usually four or five people at this point in the process. Send letters to all candidates not selected.[28]

II. Decide which Discernment Committee members will make up your Visiting Team. I recommend this being a permanent team—that is, the same people visit each candidate. This ensures that there is a basis for comparative evaluation of the candidates.

III. When selecting people to serve on a permanent Visiting Team keep in mind that 1) the team should be balanced in terms of parish representation; 2) the team will represent the congregation to prospective candidates and will communicate a great deal about your church. No more than three committee members should be sent to visit candidates. "Three persons give good balance between variety and overwhelming numbers."[29]

IV. Arrange dates and times in advance. No surprise visits! The Visiting Team needs to be sensitive to the needs of the candidates. To that end, team members should not sit together and should not take notes. The priest's congregation may or may not know that their priest is in a Discernment Process. Ask the candidate specifically how the Visiting Team should handle being at the worship service.

V. Keep in mind why you are going to visit the church. You are there to participate in the worship service, listen to the sermon, and observe how parishioners interact with their priest. You are not there to interject yourself into the life of the church. Under no circumstances is the Visiting Team to begin "interviewing" parishioners about their priest. For different reasons, answers to such questioning can be skewed. It is important to work cooperatively with candidates. This is not in any way meant to be an adversarial process.

---

28. It is good to write your own letters. Many Episcopal churches use the same sample letters and candidates have received them before so it is clear to the candidates that they are receiving a form letter.
29. The Church Deployment Board, *Caring for Clergy in the Calling Process* (New York, 1997), 14.

VI. While there, you can learn much by reading the bulletin boards, noting how the priest relates to the acolytes, noticing how little children react to the priest, noting the condition of the restrooms and sacristy.

VII. See www.shipoffools.com to see how the Mystery Worshipper reviews worship services.

VIII. Inform the candidate in advance that the Visiting Team would like to take him/her to lunch after the service, followed by a more formal time of mutual discernment. Ask prepared questions at this meeting that are the same for all candidates. It is optional whether to include the spouse or partner in the luncheon, but is not appropriate to include him/her in the meeting for mutual discernment. At the end of the meeting outline the timeline for the rest of the Discernment Committee's activities. This is very helpful to candidates and most appreciated.

IX. Keep in mind that you are involved with the pastoral care of each cleric you visit and with the care of his or her congregation.

X. The Visiting Team can fill out a copy of the evaluation sheet in Resource 13 on their way home. This data will provide you with a thorough evaluation tool and a helpful reminder when you meet with the rest of the Discernment Committee to discuss the different candidates.

Your Spiritual Guide closes the meeting.

◈ Eighth Discernment Committee Task Cluster

Your Spiritual Guide begins each of the gatherings described below.

I. When the Visiting Team has completed all visits, a recommendation is made to your Discernment Committee regarding which candidates to move forward. Again, check yourself on the "isms." Could any of your decisions be influenced by these factors? Discuss. At this point in the process, it is best to telephone candidates who are not discerned as a fit for your congregation. The caller should be prepared to give feedback as to why the candidacy is not being continued. In giving feedback, always be aware of labor laws, avoiding statements of discrimination of any kind. Be sure to check with your diocesan representative regarding the labor laws in your state.

II. Remaining candidates are invited to visit with your Discernment Committee at the church. There are many different ways to structure this time together. Note that this period of discernment usually lasts two or three days and includes the spouse/partner.[30] During this time, the candidate can meet briefly with the staff. The staff is not there to interview the candidate in any way, merely to meet them and answer questions. *Note: Some clergy may feel that more than one site visit is necessary to make a decision. It is wise to negotiate this with the candidate, especially in terms of expenses incurred.*

III. Candidates are reimbursed for all costs incurred during the Discernment Process. "Timely reimbursement of any expenses should be a priority. Meals, mileage, airport parking fees, shuttle service to the airport should all be reimbursed."[31]

IV. It is important to remember that any priest coming from outside your diocese will need to make an appointment to meet your bishop. For those coming from a distance it is important for the committee to try to set up this meeting the first time the candidate is in town. If it is put off until the final interview and the bishop is out of town or unavailable, your committee's timeline and budget could be adversely affected.

V. Set up times for the candidate, with his or her spouse if there is one, to come to the church for a tour followed by a formal meeting with the Discernment Committee. During this meeting and at all events, *committee members should wear nametags.* This tour can be tailored to the needs of the candidate, particularly with respect to whether the candidate is from outside or inside your diocese. If necessary, the tour should include the town/city and school. If housing is an issue, the candidate should be given an opportunity to view area neighborhoods as well.

VI. Prior to this meeting, review the Sixth Discernment Committee Task Cluster carefully, keeping in mind that this is a time for mutual discernment. You are not there to interview the candidates, but rather to engage in a time of discerning with them if they are called to your parish. Questions are certainly appropriate, but it is best if there is a give-and-take conversational quality to the meeting.

---

30. It is important for the Discernment Committee to be consistent. Either all spouses/partners should be invited or none should be invited. The spouse/partner is usually not included in the discernment meetings, but asking them to attend a social gathering is appropriate.
31. Vance, "Some Advice for Search Committees."

VII. Within seven days of the last candidate's visit,[32] the committee reviews the material on candidates to discern whom they believe God is calling to be their next rector or vicar. This meeting in particular should be "bathed in prayer." A priest of the committee's choosing can begin the meeting with a celebration of the Eucharist. The Discernment Committee chair can select the readings, with members leading the readings and prayers. It is important for the committee to be involved in the planning of this service.

Following the Eucharist and before any discussion takes place, at least five minutes of silent prayer is recommended in which every person prays for the ability to discern God's will for the parish. Hopefully, spiritual discernment will have taken place each step of the way, making this last time of discernment a natural next step. Even so, it is a good idea to review some of the questions raised in the Second Discernment Committee Task Cluster, urging committee members to either reflect on them silently or share in groups of two.

VIII. Within seven days of this meeting, a joint meeting between the Discernment Committee and the vestry is held in which the candidate(s) are presented to the vestry.

IX. You cannot say thank you enough to the clergy who have offered themselves to you in your Discernment Process. Be lavish in your gratitude to them. They have shared their lives with you, their hopes and dreams. Often, your final candidates will have already begun to see themselves as your rector or vicar in some way. Hearing "no" from a church where the call is truly desired will not be easy for your candidate. Sensitivity and care of each person as a child sent to you by God is needed.

X. You cannot thank yourselves and each other enough either. Your task is complete. A group celebration is in order!

---

32. It is recommended that this gathering not take place on the same day as the final candidate's meeting. A break of time is needed because of a phenomenon known as "last candidate syndrome": if the final candidates are basically equal, the last one interviewed will often receive the call, which can interfere with the process of spiritual discernment.

PART FOUR

FINAL DISCERNMENT AND CALL

◆ *Joint Vestry and Discernment Committee Meetings*

The Spiritual Guide for the Discernment Committee begins each meeting, describing the type of prayer to be used throughout.

I. The first joint meeting of the vestry and the Discernment Committee takes place before the final meeting of the candidate(s) with the vestry.[1] At this point your Transition Consultant or diocesan Transition Ministries Officer will discuss the final procedures of your diocese for calling a rector or vicar. The Transition Consultant is usually present for this meeting.

Now is also the time to begin the final background checks on your candidate(s), if you have not already done so. These may include any or all of the following checks: criminal, credit, motor vehicle, employment, sexual abuse registry.

As discussed earlier in A Note for Vestry Members, it is recommended that your wardens receive a copy of *Caring for Clergy through Compensation* and *Caring for Clergy through Housing,* which can be downloaded or ordered from www.episcopalchurch.org/cdo. In addition, if you have not already done so, obtain your diocesan compensation guidelines.

Now is the time for the Discernment Committee to share with the vestry the process it has used to discern which candidates to move forward. It is hoped that vestry members will have read *Discerning God's Will Together,* for if more than one candidate is presented, they are now called to make the final discernment. Listening to the Holy Spirit, mov-

---

1. If desired, the vestry can meet with the final candidates during the same visit as the Discernment Committee. Decide in advance which process will be followed.

ing aside any personal agendas they might have, and praying, praying, praying are of utmost importance at this critical juncture.

II. At a second joint meeting, held no more than seven days after the Discernment Committee has made its decision, the Discernment Committee presents its candidate(s) to the vestry for election.

III. The vestry then holds a meeting without the Discernment Committee present to vote on the candidate, utilizing the methods of discernment discussed earlier. If a candidate is approved and a call is extended, your wardens might consider telling the other finalists the status of the search. They will appreciate your honesty. If you wait until you extend the call to perhaps the second candidate, you might say, "We extended the call to someone else who did not feel called to our church. Now you're our number one choice."

◆ *Vestry Meeting to Elect and Extend a Call*

The vestry meets to propose to elect the new rector or vicar. At this point, the vestry can only *propose* to elect, not elect. Upon reaching a decision, the senior warden telephones the diocesan Transition Ministries Officer to communicate the results of the proposal to elect. A letter is sent to your bishop proposing the election of the candidate as rector or vicar and requesting episcopal permission to extend the call. Under canon law, your bishop has up to thirty days to respond to the proposal to elect. (See the sample "Proposal to Elect a Rector/Vicar Letter," Resource 14.)

Upon receiving permission from your bishop, the vestry meets to elect the rector or vicar and extend the call to the candidate. The Letter of Election will include the agreed start date for the rector- or vicar-elect. (See the sample "Letter of Election," Resource 15.)

For an overview of the procedure to call a rector, see your diocesan canons. See also Canon 17, Constitution and Canons of the Episcopal Church (available at www.churchpublishing.org/GC2K/).

◆ *Next Steps*

I. Background Checks
Make sure all background checks are complete.

II. The Letter of Agreement
Even if the candidate verbally agrees to become the new rector or vicar, it is not an accomplished fact until a Letter of Agreement has been signed by the candidate and the senior warden, and approved by your bishop.

It is important that the details of the written agreement be negotiated before the call is confirmed by both the candidate and the vestry. No call should be considered final until these details are discussed. Sometimes a conference call between a candidate and the wardens (or a committee appointed by the vestry for the negotiations) will clarify important issues. In the case of dual role clergy, the relation of time and effort between the nonparochial job and church duties needs to be included.

Inform the candidate that she/he is allowed up to one week in which to reflect and pray about the decision, and then to communicate his or her discernment by telephone. If a candidate requests more than one week, the committee might want to consider carefully the motives for the request.

If the candidate does not discern a call to the parish, the Discernment Committee and the vestry need to take time to reflect upon what happened and to make any necessary adjustments in their expectations or changes in their process. It can be painful when this happens, and the pastoral concern of the interim and/or the bishop or bishop's staff may be needed. *Patience is required at this point. Standards for a choice must not be lowered. Do not automatically assume the runner-up should be recommended.*

Upon acceptance of the call and the signing of the Letter of Agreement by the rector- or vicar-elect and the senior warden, the senior warden has the responsibility to get the Letter of Agreement to the bishop for approval.

III. Communication
The details and timing of the announcement are very important. This cannot occur until the Letter of Agreement has been approved by your bishop and should occur in conjunction with desires of the rector- or vicar-elect. There needs to be sensitivity toward the priest's current congregation so they do not hear about this announcement from any other source than the rector- or vicar-elect.

After the Letter of Agreement has been signed and approved, the Discernment Committee must notify all other candidates promptly, either by telephone or in writing. A telephone call is recommended at this stage in the process. It has unfortunately happened on a number of occasions that remaining candidates are not informed that someone else has been called. As one candidate stated, "It is very disheartening to believe you have had a positive discussion with a committee, to not hear anything for several months, then to read in *The Living Church* that they have called someone else!" Candidates not chosen may ask the Discernment Committee for feedback about not being selected. This is entirely appropriate and the committee is encouraged to be open, being mindful that *any explanation needs to be consistent with labor laws.*

IV. Discharging the Discernment Committee

The Discernment Committee is to be honored for their dedicated work on behalf of your congregation. Their discernment is now finished. At a Sunday morning worship service, the vestry formally discharges the Discernment Committee of their duties and thanks them profusely.

At this point, all Discernment Committee records, notes, and personal clergy profile evaluations are destroyed.

V. Preparing for a New Rector/Vicar

The vestry now gathers all the necessary information that a new rector or vicar might need. (See "Survival Kit for a New Rector/Vicar," Resource 16.)

RESOURCES FOR THE DISCERNMENT PROCESS

Resources 1, 2, and 3 are included here; Resources 17, 18, and 19 may be found within the chapters. All of the Resources may be downloaded from www.churchpublishing.org/callingclergy.

Resource 1
RESOURCES FOR YOUR SPIRITUAL GUIDE

Serving as the Spiritual Guide for your Self-Study or Discernment Committee is an honor and a sacred responsibility. You have been chosen because your peers see something special in you, sense that you can guide them through this significant time of discernment and transition in the life of your parish. You already have what you need or you would not have been chosen. My hope is to give you some extra tools to add to your own to help you fulfill the responsibilities that lie before you.

First, your own devotional style is the best place to start. How do you pray? How do you make decisions? Relating how you pray and make decisions will be helpful to those who have asked you to serve in this role. In addition, I hope that you have read *Discerning God's Will Together: A Spiritual Practice for the Church* by Danny E. Morris and Charles M. Olsen and that you have gleaned new ideas related to decision-making in groups. This book can be used to inform the decision-making that will occur in your committee.

In *Transforming Church Boards into Communities of Spiritual Leaders,* Charles M. Olsen outlines specific prayer methods that can transform vestries and other church committees into spiritual communities. Most of us are familiar with what he calls "book-end prayers"—praying at the beginning and end of a meeting. This type of prayer is of limited use, relegating the spiritual as separate and distinct from the "business" of the meeting. Instead, he suggests turning meetings into "worshipful work" in which prayer is used throughout. While serving as chaplain to several regional and national conferences, I have used methods one through four outlined below with positive results and commend them to you.

1. Rotate prayer: At the beginning of the meeting, give one person a sacred object like Anglican rosary beads, a cross, or a symbol of your church. Ask him/her to hold it and pray for approximately five to ten minutes, or for as long as the Spirit moves. When through, she/he can silently pass the object to the person next to him/her so that person can begin to pray. During their time of prayer, they can pray for each person on the committee as well as about what is being discussed.

At the end of the gathering, ask members what it felt like: a) to pray silently during the meeting; b) to know that someone was praying at all times. I have witnessed nothing less than the transformation of group discussion by using this simple method of prayer. In large groups, three to four objects can be passed around simultaneously.

2. Gleaning prayer: As chaplain, without telling other participants, I have kept four lists during a meeting—for thanksgivings, intercessions, petitions, and works of the Spirit of God.[1] As conversation unfolds, I fill in the lists based on the type of prayer that would aid in the subject discussed. At the end of the gathering, a meaningful prayer is given that sums up all that occurred as well as sets it within the context of prayer. It is difficult to describe the power of this type of prayer and the effect on conference participants or committee members. Try it! For another gathering, you might want to ask four different people to be involved, each keeping one list and offering their prayers at the end.

3. Offer prayers of confession: "Naming 'how things really are' and 'what is left undone' are healthy processes for a board," writes Olsen.[2] How refreshing this would be for a Self-Study or Discernment Committee! With this work in particular, conflict can arise for a multitude of reasons. Naming it, by naming how things really are, can help a committee move beyond it. As Spiritual Guide you may be the right person to bring up such topics. Doing so within the understanding of confession can begin to turn a situation of conflict into a situation of healing.

4. Draw upon model prayers of scripture: Consider the psalms, the Lord's Prayer, Jesus' prayer for his friends in John 17, and Paul's heartfelt prayer of thanksgiving for his friends in Philippians 1:3–11.[3]

5. Committee prayers: Ask a different committee member to write a prayer to be used at critical times in the next committee meeting. When needed, stop the meeting and call for this prayer to be read.

6. Time for reflection: Study the reflection chapters in this book ahead of time and plan to discuss them with committee members at the meeting that follows.

7. Spiritual support: Above all, make sure you have the spiritual support you need either from your interim, a trained spiritual director, or a spiritual friend. Keeping you own spiritual house in order is critical to being able to lead others.

1. Charles M. Olsen, *Transforming Church Boards into Communities of Spiritual Leaders* (Virginia: The Alban Institute, Inc., 1995), 21.
2. Olsen, *Transforming Church Boards,* 21–22.
3. Olsen, *Transforming Church Boards,* 23.

8. *Use the Book of Common Prayer often:* It holds within its pages some of the most beautiful prayers ever written and they are there for you to use lavishly. Some suggested prayers are: "For the Church," "For the Mission of the Church," "For Clergy and People," and "For the Parish" (BCP 816–817); "For the Election of a Bishop or other Minister" and "For the Unity of the Church" (BCP 818); both prayers "For Guidance," and "For Quiet Confidence" (BCP 832); the collects for Advent (BCP 211–212); "Of a Pastor" (BCP 248); "For All Christians in their Vocation" and "For the Mission of the Church" (BCP 256–257); and "For Vocation in Daily Work" (BCP 261) Add your own favorites or those of particular relevance to your committee's discussions.

9. *Use the prayers below from* Women's Uncommon Prayers:[4]

For Leaders
Almighty God, you have given us the responsibility for the leadership of the Church for a season. Grant us patience, courage, and wisdom to discern your will amidst the many competing claims and conflicts of this present time. Give us an appreciative memory for all who have gone before, and a strong clear vision of the church of the future. Let us exercise our stewardship with energy and enthusiasm, so that, when the time comes, we may joyfully relinquish our tasks to those who come after. We ask this in the name of our redeemer, Jesus Christ, who calls us into fellowship and sends the Holy Spirit to guide and inspire us, generation after generation, that we may do all to your greater glory. Amen.
                                        —Dr. Pamela P. Chinnis

For Times of Change
Assist us, Lord, in living hopefully into the future. In the face of change, help us to set unnecessary fears aside and to recognize our potential for creative response. Help us to develop a reasonable optimism when confronted by "the new" and to guard us against our own defensiveness. Be with us as we remember and celebrate former times, and keep us from unreasonable yearning for them, which takes us from the work you have set before us in our time. All this we ask in the name of your Child, our savior, Jesus Christ. Amen.
                                        —The Reverend Linda C. Smith-Criddle

---

4. Elizabeth Rankin Geitz, Marjorie A. Burke, and Ann Smith, eds., *Women's Uncommon Prayers* (Harrisburg: Morehouse Publishing, 2000), 362–363. Used with permission.

Resource 2
LEADER'S GUIDE FOR FOCUS GROUP
MEETINGS TO DEVELOP PROFILE[1]

Putting the Groups Together
The goal is to secure the participation of as many people as possible in the Discernment Process; even if the profile does not ultimately reflect exactly what one person wants, she/he has had a voice in the process. How this is best accomplished is going to have local variations. This exercise will take about one and a half hours. When you announce your plans, be sure people know that you want them to stay for the entire event, and that this is the way in which they can participate in and guide the Discernment Committee, so it's very important!

Self-Study Committees have had success with both of the following Focus Group plans; use whichever one best suits the culture of your congregation.

1. Schedule a series of "cottage" meetings, either in the evenings or on Saturday or Sunday afternoons, in people's homes or even in the church. Encourage folks to participate with people they don't know as well (call it a fellowship opportunity) and, where possible, encourage family members to attend different meetings—they benefit from the broader experience, too. If possible, limit the size of the group to eight participants, plus the facilitators. Twelve is the maximum number you should allow. *Or*

2. Schedule a meeting on one or two Sundays immediately after the main service. Use an expanded coffee hour as a "hook" (in other words, more food!) and provide childcare for the youngest children. Give each person a number, randomly, to break the group into manageable "roundtables" for discussion. These discussions work best if groups are limited to eight to twelve people; members of the same family should be in different groups to encourage full freedom of individual expression.

In both of the above plans, two people working together should facilitate each Focus Group. At least one should be a member of the Self-Study Committee. You can help keep each other on track, help move the process along, and spell each other as "scribe" on a computer or newsprint. Be sure to identify in advance who will lead which portion of the Focus Group meeting so that you work together smoothly as a team.

---

1. Written by the Rev. Dr. Molly Dale Smith. Used with permission.

SUPPLIES NEEDED   Laptop computer, LCD projector and screen, or
                       newsprint
                       Several magic markers; black is easiest to read
                       Pencils and small pads of paper, one for each
                       participant

I. WELCOME AND PURPOSE (10 MINUTES)

*Welcome the participants; encourage them to sit comfortably where everyone
can see the screen or newsprint, and the leaders. Give any "housekeeping"
information such as where the coffee is, or where the bathroom is located
(especially important for "cottage" meetings).*

*Remind everyone why you have gathered: to gather information about your
church today, and where you would like your church to be in the next three to
five years:*

> The process we will use is a variation on something called "brainstorm-
> ing." (Some, if not all, will be familiar with this process.) Brainstorming
> is a technique to pool the ideas of a group quickly. It is intended to
> involve everyone's participation. We will use this process to get your
> input on six specific areas of parish life, the four pastoral or ministry
> skills we believe to be most needed at this time in the life of the con-
> gregation, and, finally, a general assessment of where we are and
> where we want to go.

Hand out pencils and paper.

> The reason for giving you pencils and paper is that you may well have
> a thought that you want to contribute, but it's on a different topic than
> the one we're on at the moment. Please write it down, so that we can
> capture it when we're on that topic, or get back to it at the end of the
> agenda.

II. THE AGENDA

*You may wish to have the agenda projected on your screen or as the first sheet
of newsprint, or you may wish to write it out as you speak. You may also want
to hand out a copy to participants so they can see what's coming up.*

A. Ground Rules for Discussion
B. Our Parish Life
   1. Ministry of the Laity
   2. Liturgical/Spiritual Life
   3. Educational Life
   4. Evangelism and Renewal

5. Outreach
6. Stewardship
C. Gifts We Seek in Our Next Rector/Vicar
D. Hopes and Dreams
E. General Parish Assessment

A. *Ground Rules for Discussion*

* All ideas and thoughts are acceptable.
* There are no right or wrong answers.
* This is not a debate, but rather a free-flowing sharing of our individual thoughts. No analysis, comments, or criticisms allowed.
* Repetition is okay; it may spark a new idea. Ideas build on one another.
* One person speaks at a time.
* Only questions for clarity are allowed.

As leaders, hold the participants to these ground rules. You may want to post them or hand them out. It is your responsibility both to control the group so one or two voices do not dominate and to encourage everyone's participation.

B. *Our Parish Life*

As you introduce each category, make a brief statement or raise a series of questions that guide the ideas. For each of the six areas, ask the same two questions: 1) Where are we presently? 2) Where do we want to be three to five years from today?

1. Ministry of the Laity
   Current: Where are we today? Do we have a variety of opportunities for lay ministry or not? Do we do any training for lay ministry? What do we do in our small group meetings— social, study, etc.? Where is our leadership focused? *(2 minutes)*
   Future: What would we like to add or do differently? Where do we want to be three to five years from today? *(3 minutes)*
2. Liturgical/Spiritual Life
   Current: What are our services like? How do we participate? What is our view of our prayer and spiritual life? How do we help our membership in this area? *(2 minutes)*
   Future: What would we like to change and how? Where do we want to be three to five years from today? *(3 minutes)*

3. Educational Life

Current: What do we do now? When? What do we emphasize: scripture, Anglican studies, contemporary issues, etc.? When does our education take place? Is it mostly for children, or mostly for adults? *(2 minutes)*
Future: What would we like to change or add? Where do we want to be three to five years from today? *(3 minutes)*

4. Evangelism and Renewal

Current: Do we reach out beyond our church to bring in new people? How? Do we welcome new members? How? Who does the reaching out to newcomers? How? *(2 minutes)*
Future: What would we like to change? Where do we want to be three to five years from today? *(3 minutes)*

5. Outreach

Current: How do we interact with our diocese? How do we use our buildings and facilities? Do we support programs outside of ourselves? How well do we work with people in other denominations or faith traditions? *(2 minutes)*
Future: What would we like to change? Do differently? Where do we want to be three to five years from today? *(3 minutes)*

6. Stewardship

Current: Do our leaders teach and practice stewardship, including proportional giving toward the tithe? Does our stewardship include talents/gifts as well as financial stewardship? Who teaches about stewardship? How is stewardship taught? *(2 minutes)*
Future: What would we like to change or do differently? Where do we want to be three to five years from today? *(3 minutes)*

Summary

Does anyone have anything to add to any of the categories that you noted, but we didn't capture? *(Add as needed.)*

This is a good point for a brief break; people have been working hard.

C. Gifts We Seek in Our Next Rector/Vicar

List the twenty-one ministry skills identified by the Church Deployment Office on newsprint. (You can do this ahead of time.) Then clarify what each term means, if necessary.

- Administration
- Christian Formation/Education

- Church Growth/Development
- Communications Ministry
- Consulting/Transition Ministry

- Music Ministry
- Outreach/Social Justice Advocacy
- Pastoral Care
- Preaching
- Spiritual Guidance

- Counseling
- Ecumenical/Interfaith
- Evangelism
- Leadership Development
- Liturgy
- Multi-/Cross-Cultural Ministry

- Stewardship
- Teaching
- Theology
- Ministry with Youth
- Other

Ask people to make a checkmark or a dot by each of the six skills that are most important to them. (This exercise should take about ten minutes.)

D. Hopes and Dreams

Brainstorm for about ten to fifteen minutes (at most) on dreams and what you might do to get there. Brainstorming rules apply!

E. General Parish Assessment

Report results to participants.

Resource 3
ADDITIONAL FOCUS GROUP INFORMATION[1]

TRAINING GROUP LEADERS

"Leaders do not need answers; leaders must have the right questions." —Church Leadership, Saint Paul School of Theology

WHAT:
> *The goal of the group*
> - Fill in gaps found in the congregational survey.
> - Complete Parish Search Request form.
> - Each person participates in the process.

WHEN:
> *Timing or format*
> - Workshop/retreat design.
> - Several sessions with the same group. *(60 minutes each)*
> - Several one-time sessions with different groups of people.

WHO:
> *Participants in the group*
> - Whoever comes.
> - Persons invited to represent different constituencies.
> - An established group if this is a special program.
> - Large number to be subdivided into smaller groups.
> *Size*
> - Optimum group size is ten.
> - If twelve people are present, divide into two groups.

WHERE:
> *The setting*
> - At church, in homes.
> - Comfortable chairs and temperature are essential.
> - Refreshments are helpful.
> - Know the culture and what works in your congregation.

HOW:
> *The Agenda*
> - Follow the plan provided.
> - Create your own agenda.
> *The Recorder*
> - Someone, not the leader, MUST be responsible for recording all information.

1. Written by the Rev. Dr. Molly Dale Smith.

SAMPLE MEETING OUTLINE

1. Opening Prayer *(2 minutes)*
Use the prayer being used for the church on Sunday mornings.

2. Introduction *(5 to 15 minutes)*
Introduce yourself briefly.
Icebreaker: Ask each person to tell the following:
                           • What is your name?
                           • What about this church excites you most?
                           • What about this church energizes you?
Review the agenda.

3. Meeting Plan

SAMPLE AGENDA
PRIMARY GOAL   To obtain information for the Parish Search
                        Request Form

I. Parish Search Request Form of the Episcopal Church *(5 minutes)*
     • What the form is.
     • How it is used.
     • How the form works: includes both present and future.

II. Exploring our Mission *(50 minutes)*
     a. Brainstorm the single word that best describes the mission of this
     church: outreach, worship, music, Christian education, etc. *(5 minutes)*
     b. List all the words on whiteboard.
     c. Divide into groups of four and pick the top four words. Write one sen-
     tence about what each means for your congregation. *(15 minutes)*
     d. As a large group make one list of your top four words. *(10 minutes)*
     e. Spend five minutes on each of the top four words in terms of what
     they mean for your church. *(20 minutes)*

III. Ministry Specialties *(27 minutes)*
     a. Describe the Responsibilities category of the Search Request Form.
     (5 minutes)
     b. The group picks its ten most important categories. *(7 minutes)*
     c. Now the group ranks the ten categories in order of importance.
     (7 minutes)
     d. The group chooses the four most important categories. *(3 minutes)*
     e. The group is shown the list of the four top-ranked ministry special-
     ties determined from the survey *(the list is already written on white-
     board)*, then, using this information, chooses again the four
     Responsibility categories. *(5 minutes)*

IV. Closing Prayer *(2 minutes)*
   Thank all participants. Lead the Lord's Prayer.

V. Closing Up
   Be sure to collect all papers and written materials.

   Total time: 95 to 115 minutes

TEN GUIDELINES FOR A SMALL GROUP LEADER

1. Pray before the meeting
   • Pray for the people who will be participating in the meeting, by name if possible.
   • Pray that the meeting goal will be achieved.
   • Pray for the guidance of the Holy Spirit for yourself and for the participants.

2. Prepare
   • Room arrangement: seating, temperature.
   • Materials: Paper and pencils if needed. Handouts? Newsprint and masking tape? Preprinted information?
   • Task: What is your goal and how do you expect to achieve the goal?
   • Timing: Plan each step so that the goal may be achieved in the available time.
   • Relationships: How will you help people feel cared for? What can you do to break the ice? To relax, feel comfortable, open up?

3. Start on time
   • Don't wait for latecomers.

4. Set a tone of friendly openness
   • Introduce yourself. Use an icebreaker, if needed.
   • Establish an atmosphere of love and encouragement.

5. Present and clarify the agenda at the beginning
   • Discuss purpose and method (how purpose will be achieved).

6. Recognize every person as important
   • Seek to gain everyone's participation in the group.
   • Let them know that their ideas and comments are valued.

7. Summarize progress from time to time
   • This will help keep the group on track and is a way to keep moving toward your goal.

8. Guide more than direct
  • The leader is a facilitator, not the authority or teacher.
  • Don't be afraid of silence.

9. Stop on time and on a positive note
  • Even if you have not achieved your purpose you must stop on time. The only exception is if the entire group really does want to continue. Then contract to continue for a specific amount of time and then you must stop.

10. Thank them for coming
  • This ends the meeting on a good tone.

OTHER NOTES

A. On-the-job training
  • Many people will have group leader experience from other parts of their life.

B. The recorder
  • Best if this person is another member of the Self-Study Committee.
  • Collects all newsprint and other notes taken, as well as her or his own notes.

C. Use of PowerPoint, whiteboard, or newsprint
  • Using whiteboard, newsprint, or PowerPoint helps keeps the entire group on task.
  • Any newsprint to be used by the leader should be written on in advance. Why? To avoid wasting time and to make sure the writing is clear and legible.

D. Value of tight structure: LESS IS MORE
  • People work better on this kind of task with *less* not more time. They are forced to use their intuition and refrain from getting bogged down.
  • There will probably be much grumbling that there is not enough time but that will dissipate.
  • The leaders will function more comfortably with a clearly defined agenda.
  • It is crucial that all groups follow the same agenda in order to compare results.

CPSIA information can be obtained
at www.ICGtesting.com
Printed in the USA
FSHW021820151119
64083FS